598

NEW WAYS WITH MACRAMÉ

NEW WAYS WITH
MACRAMÉ

Joyce Hargreaves

Sketches by Joyce Hargreaves
Photographs and diagrams by Brian Hargreaves

Larousse & Co., Inc. New York, N.Y.

Dedication

To our parents

All projects and ceramics unless otherwise
stated have been designed and executed by
Joyce Hargreaves

First published 1981
© Brian and Joyce Hargreaves 1981

ISBN 0-88332-264-1

LC 81-81036

Printed in Great Britain

Contents

List of colour photographs 7

Acknowledgements 8

1 **Introduction** 10

2 **Macramé Materials** 13
Yarns 13
Lengths and Widths of Cord 15
A Butterfly Bobbin 15
Workshop Materials 16

3 **Macramé Techniques** 19
The Start and the Finish 20
The Square Knot and Its Variations 21
Cording 23
Wrap Knots and Tassels 25
Decorative Knots 26
Working in the Round 28
Colour 29

4 **Working in Leather** 30
Types of Leather and Tools 30
Knotting with Thonging 31
Laminated Leather 32

5 **Clay and Ceramic Techniques** 34
Types of Clay and Firing Techniques: 34
earthenware and terracotta – stoneware –
porcelain – raku – cold clay
Hand-built Methods: 38
coil pot – slab-built tabletop – shell-shaped
saucer dish
Lino Relief Decoration 40

6 **Making Papier Mâché** 43
Paper Pulp 43
Constructing Papier Mâché Shapes: 44
reproducing an existing shape – creating a
new form using an armature
Decoration and Finishes 48

7 **Serendipity** 51
Objets Trouvés: 51
the ready-made object – the natural object
Charity Shops and Bazaars 54
Craftwork from Other Countries 56

8 **Beads** 57
Types of Bead: 60
china and glass beads – plastic beads –
wooden beads – beads from natural materials
**Making Ceramic, Cold Clay, Papier
Mâché and Paper Beads:** 62
press moulding
The Uses of Hand-made Beads 64
Attaching Beads to Macramé 64

9 **Jewellery** 67
**Incorporating Different Media into the
Macramé Jewellery** 67
**Project: Turk's Head Torc Necklace
and Bracelet –** 68
Made in Papier Mâché and Macramé
materials – method

10 **Garments** 72
Suitable Materials 72
**Project: Chinese Harlequin
Waistcoat –** 74
Made in Leather
materials – method

11 Accessories 79

Day and Evening Wear and Animal
Accessories 79

Project I: Sioux Belt and Pouch – 80
Made in Wool (or Jute) and Leather
materials – method

Project II: Horse's Fly Fringe – 85
Made in Cotton Twine:
materials – method

**12 Plant Hangings, Wind-chimes
and Bells 87**

Combining Plants, Pots and Macramé 87

Bells 89

Wind-chimes 89

Project I: Geisha Plant Pot Hanging – 90
Made in Cord with a Variety of Pots:
materials – method

Project II: Daisy Chain Saucer Hanging 92
– Made in Ceramic, or Papier Mâché
and Wool:
materials – method – the daisies

Project III: Wind-chime 94

13 Hanging Tables and Dishes 95

Design of Hanging Tables 95

Wood and Papier Mâché Tabletops 97

Project: Crystal Palace Hanging Table – 98
Made in Ceramic, Wood or Papier
Mâché and Cord:
materials – method

14 Macramé as an Art Form 101

Wall Hangings 101

Mobiles 103

Sculptures 107

Art Forms and Other Media 107

Project: 'Draco', a Dragon Mobile – 107
Made in Wire and Cotton Twine:
materials – method

Glossary 116

Suppliers 118

Index 119

List of colour photographs

between pages 48 and 49

1 An African mask made of clay with a head-dress that incorporates macramé and other media

2 The girl's waistcoat, the dog's lead and the horse's fly fringe all demonstrate different uses of macramé

3 This necklace is knotted in macramé twine and decorated with glass beads and shells

between pages 72 and 73

4 'Hampton Court', a wall hanging

5 A group of plant hangings includes containers made of ceramics, papier mâché and shells

6 A table hanging which combines white cord and a ceramic tabletop

Acknowledgements

My thanks go to my father, Mr S. J. Soar, for checking the manuscript and to Misses Deborah Slinn and Deborah Le Marquand and Mrs R. Arora for modelling the garments and jewellery. I particularly wish to thank Mr Michael Bolton for designing the silver jewellery shapes and also for loaning two superb silver and gold pendants to incorporate into macramé settings. Thanks also to all my friends and relatives who have provided me with a varied supply of beads and other materials.

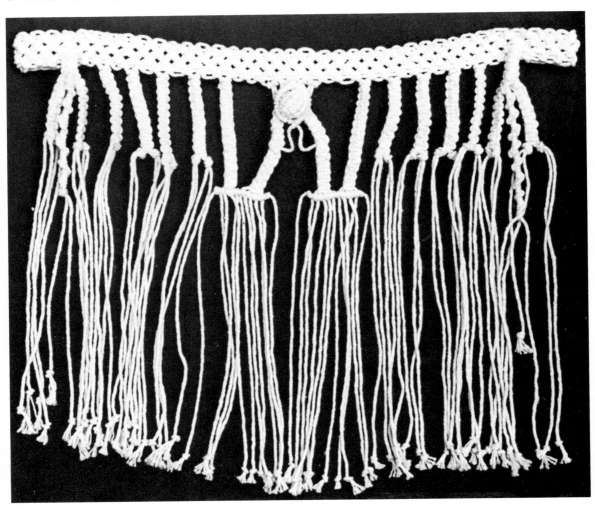

1 Introduction

It is not known when macramé, the art of decorative knotting, was first discovered. The answer must lie in pre-history, for it would seem likely that cavemen entwined pieces of fibrous vegetation together to enable them to carry their simply constructed pots and other heavy articles. We do know, however, that in the thirteenth century macramé knotting was used in Arabia and by the fifteenth century sailors were using macramé articles for barter. Seafaring men used to knot both useful and saleable articles to pass the time on board ship during long sea voyages and, while travelling around the world, they gleaned and spread ideas from many sources. No doubt the complex knotting techniques that we know today were derived from these much travelled matelots.

Mary, the wife of William of Orange, was believed to have introduced macramé into Great Britain in the seventeenth century, and by Victorian times it was widely used for making a variety of dainty, lace-like fringes. By the early twentieth century a simpler life style had evolved, elaborate fringes and chair backs were no longer fashionable, and knotting became one of the least known and used crafts.

Today macramé has again come into favour after its long decline and with its return has come a subtle change from the intricate knotting beloved by the Victorians. Modern interpretations of the old techniques express creativity, individuality and the endeavour

A small hanging knotted in rayon fishing twine and trimmed with two oriental china beads. It supports three clove oranges and would make a fragrant addition to a wardrobe

to generate an evocative atmosphere by using and combining unusual materials. While keeping in mind the textural quality of the knots, the trend today is turned away from pure cord compositions and towards incorporating found objects, ceramics, beads and many other complementary articles into both utilitarian and aesthetic creations. This probably brings the craft much nearer to its original form when primitive people first tied long grasses together and maybe even decorated their results with holed pebbles and animal teeth.

It was on the occasion when I added a few decorative pots to a kilnful of ceramic sculpture that I was making that first led me to use macramé. These pots clearly needed

---

This torn and cut paper collage 'Lucrezia Borgia' includes a macramé head-dress knotted in cording, square and overhand knots

A monkey's fist knot tied on the end of a coil of rope to give it weight when it is flung from a ship onto a quay

including leather, that can be used. The last part of the book describes how to combine macramé with these other media to make useful and decorative articles.

Instructions for making a number of projects are also included. Some of these projects, for example the two plant hangings, are very simple to make, while the hanging table and the dragon mobile are designed for the more advanced knotter. These projects will, I hope, stimulate you to think and make use of some of the many kinds of seemingly unrelated objects that can embellish the individualistic techniques of macramé.

hangings and so I obtained a book of knots and some cord and set to work. As the hangings grew so did my enthusiasm for this versatile craft. I began to experiment by making, finding and buying a number of different objects that could be successfully added to macramé either to complement the knotting or to co-exist on equal terms with it. Here are the results of these experiments which, I hope, will help you to make or select suitable objects that, when combined with macramé, will contribute handsomely towards the quality of your finished projects.

Chapters later in this book on ceramics and papier mâché show how it is possible to make pots, dishes and tabletops that can easily be incorporated into macramé hangings. Many of the designs shown here do not require expert knowledge of the craft involved or expensive equipment, and there is advice for those who prefer to select their adjuncts to macramé from the range of goods available in the shops. There are instructions too for making beads and when and how to use the many different types of bought bead which are so easy to obtain nowadays.

Found objects knotted into a piece of macramé often give life and vitality to it and in the chapter on serendipity there is advice on where to go and what to look for in your search for interesting items of objet trouvé.

Naturally there are instructions for tying the knots themselves and for the techniques of making macramé easy to handle, as well as information on the types of material,

Some examples of macramé mixed with other media. The boy wears a jute and leather pouch and the girl's belt is made of ceramic plaques held together with chinese crown knots. She wears a necklace knotted in waxed twine and decorated with found objects; her bracelet is made of macramé and papier mâché

12

2 Macramé Materials

The basic requirements of macramé are a pair of hands, some yarn and a knowledge of the knots, and it is the simplicity of the materials required for knotting that makes this craft so attractive. As macramé requires, first of all, yarn, one of the prime considerations is the selection of suitable types of fibres. The textural quality of an article and its successful completion will depend on this.

Yarns

The types of fibre suitable for macramé come under three headings.

Vegetable fibres

Some of the most popular macramé yarns are made from vegetable fibres. Cotton, obtained from the cotton plant, comes in many forms and thicknesses. Cotton is one of the easiest materials to work with, especially good quality white twine and dish-cloth yarn. Jute, which comes from the inner bark of the tall corchorus plant, is another popular fibre, but it is not rot-proof and is inclined to shed its fibres during knotting. Linen is one of the oldest natural fibres and is harvested from the flax plant. It gives a soft smooth texture to the work and a good knot definition, but is also another material that sheds its fibres. Sisal, obtained from the fleshy, blade-like leaves of *Agave sisalana*, is the commonest form of packaging string and makes an inexpensive macramé yarn.

A triple plant hanging. The macramé hanging is knotted with purple cotton, white silk and natural jute twisted together to form a single cord. The effect resembles tweed

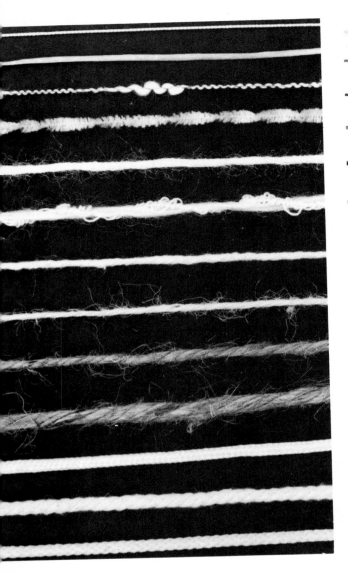

Cords on the black card
1 Fine rayon thread
2 Waxed nylon thread
3 Coton neige decorative wool
4 Chenille
5 Silk
6 Decorative knitting wool
7 Fine cotton twine
8, 9, 10 Three thicknesses of jute
11 Nylon picture cord
12 Heavy cotton twine
13 Nylon/polyester rot-proof cord

Cords on the white card
1 Polypropylene
2 Macramé twine
3, 4, 5, 6 Four thicknesses of terylene fishing twine
7 Embroidery cotton
8 Dish-cloth cotton
9 American cotton twine
10 Terylene marine cord
11 Rayon cord
12 Two fold woollen spun
13 Silk
14 Linen/viscose cord

Animal fibres

Wool is the animal fibre commonly used for knotting. It is soft, lightweight and warm but only some types are suitable for knotting. Wool has a tendency to stretch so the best types to use are rug and other non-elastic kinds of wool. Unspun fleece can also be used for textural interest. Silk is a very beautiful animal fibre that can look most attractive when used in macramé. It is costly but the result generally justifies the expense.

Synthetics

There are many kinds of synthetic fibres obtainable and most of these man-made yarns are suitable for macramé knotting. Rayon is a luxurious, shiny yarn but not one to be recommended to the inexperienced knotter as it is slippery, difficult to manage and unravels easily. Nylon/polyester and terylene are easier to manage and have the advantage of being rot-proof and unpalatable to insects, which means that articles made in these materials can be safely left outdoors. Chenille, made of acrylic fibres, gives a rich, velvety texture to any work knotted in it. Metallic cords are useful for jewellery and polypropylene, which is obtainable in a wide range of colours, is especially useful for plant and table hangings.

Lengths and Widths of Cord

Although yarn is usually described by its ply (3-ply, 5-ply, etc.) ply refers to the number of strands that are twisted into the cord and bears no relation to its size. Cord sizes are described in terms of their diameter.

When cords are mounted at their centres, on a project, the cords need to be at least eight times the length of the work when the knots are simply and loosely tied. Cording and other tightly knotted work will require cords about ten or more times the length of the finished article.

A Butterfly Bobbin

When working with long cords it is necessary to loop up the ends for ease of working. The best way to do this is to tie a butterfly bobbin. To make a butterfly bobbin wrap the cord in a figure of eight between the thumb and the index finger (diagram 1). When most of the cord is taken up the bundle is confined by an elastic band. Lengths of cord can then be pulled out as needed from the rubber band.

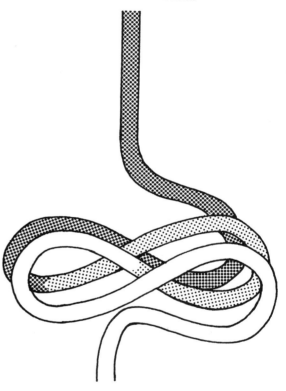

Diagram 1 **How to form a butterfly bobbin**

Workshop Materials

Working boards

Although there are very few workshop
materials needed for macramé there are
some that can be of assistance to a macramé
worker. It is often difficult to tie a piece of
macramé without using a working board of
some sort as a support. Sometimes the
whole article requires to be pinned to a
board, or perhaps only a decorative and
complex knot needs to be pinned into
position.

In Victorian times gentlewomen made their
elaborate fringes with cords that were
pinned to a velvet cushion on a wooden
base. Today there are many different
materials that can be used in place of this
complicated clamped cushion and board.
The working board can be made of any stiff
material that can have a pin pushed easily
into it and does not have a fibrous surface
that will come off on the work in progress.
Suitable materials can also include soft
board which has been painted or covered
with plastic. The size of the board will
depend on the object that is being made on
it: large for a garment, small for a few knots.

Other supports

It does not always require a working board
to support a piece of macramé. Belts and
other similar articles can be fastened at one
end to a drawer or cupboard handle and it is
much easier to knot the article when it is
under tension at one end like this. Large
projects like bead curtains, hanging tables
and room dividers are too big to be pinned
to a board. In order to knot them
successfully and also to ascertain that they
hang properly it is a good idea to support
the hanging from the top of a door and work
on it whilst it hangs in the doorway.

Pins

The macramé is attached to the working
board by pins and again the size of the pin

Above:
A poncho that opens at the back is pinned to a working board

Right:
This piece of a pomander hanging was knotted in terylene fishing cord

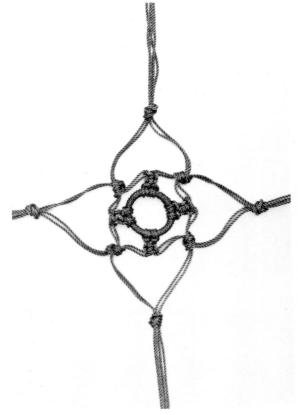

will depend on the size of the article being knotted. Generally two pin sizes will be sufficient, glass-headed pins for smaller pieces and heavier T-shaped pins for 5-ply heavy cords.

Adhesives

Often cords have to be tucked into the back of a piece of macramé and it is safer if they can be glued into position. For the simple fastening off of a cord the adhesive need not be very strong but needs to be as invisible as possible. I use a very small amount of UHU glue (American equivalent: Sobo cement) for this purpose. Often when wrapping an object with cord it makes the wrap stronger if the surface to be wrapped also has a smear of glue over it.

3 Macramé Techniques

In order to understand the technique of knotting it is necessary to be familiar with this short glossary of terms which are nearly always self explanatory. (There is a more complete general glossary at the end of the book.)

Sinnet   A chain of successive knots

Working cords   The cords used for tying the knots

Filler cords   The cords around which the knots are tied

Leader cords   The knot-bearing cords used in horizontal and diagonal cording

Foundation cords   The mounting cords used to support the working and filler cords

Floating cords   The loose cords that are not knotted

There are only two basic knots to be found in macramé, one is the square knot and the other is the half hitch. These two knots form the basis of all macramé work but there are, of course, many variations of these knots and also a wide variety of other knots which can be useful to a competent macramé worker.

In this chapter I have described only the knots necessary for making the projects which occur later in this book. For a comprehensive vocabulary of knots *The Ashley book of Knots* or Raoul M. Graumond's *Encyclopedia of Knots* are to be recommended.

'Nightfall' shows cording, bannister bars, square knots and tassels

The Start and the Finish

The usual way to start a piece of macramé is to pin a foundation cord onto a working board and fasten the working and filler cords to it using a lark's head knot. Diagram 2 shows how it should be tied. If the knot is reversed it is known as a reversed lark's head knot and is used when the loop on the front of the pattern is not wanted.

The simplest knot in macramé is the overhand knot and the method of tying it is shown in diagram 3. Although it is such a simple knot it is most useful and versatile. It serves to tie off ends and prevent unravelling, it can be used to anchor a knot-bearing cord, to hold small items in position, or just as decoration. It can also be used as an ornamental mounting if it is tied to a cord at its centre before the cord is clove-hitched to a foundation cord.

Multiples of this knot (see diagram 4) form a coil knot which makes a heavier and more decorative finish to a hanging cord.

Coil knots decorate the bottom of a plant hanging

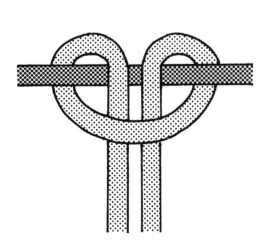

Diagram 2

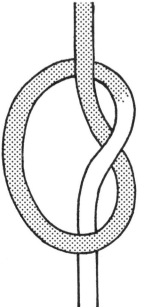

Diagram 3

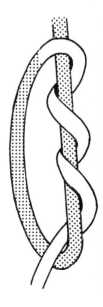

Diagram 4

The Square Knot and Its Variations

The square knot or flat knot is made up of two opposing half knots. Diagram 5 shows how to tie a half knot and diagram 6 shows a square knot. Usually four cords are used; two outer working cords are knotted over two inner filler cords. These can be tied in sinnets or worked into an alternate square knot pattern.

Alternate square knot pattern

To alternate square knots move the knot two cords over in alternate rows so that the knot falls below the space in the preceding row. This pattern diagram 7 can have an open, net-like appearance or a woven texture, depending on how tightly it is knotted.

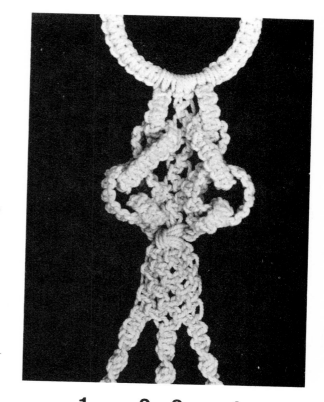

The top of a hanging table shows many of the square knot variations described here

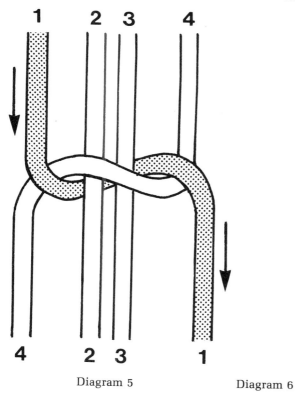

Diagram 5

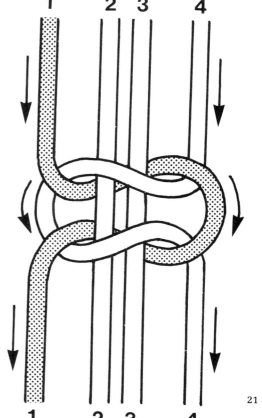

Diagram 6

The bannister bar (or twisted sinnet)

As can be seen from the diagrams 5 and 6 the square knot is made up of two half knots. If a sinnet is worked with a series of half knots it will have a natural twist either to the left or to the right depending upon which half of the square knot is used. This sinnet is called a bannister bar or a twisted sinnet.

The triple knot

A triple knot will give the work extra firmness. It is tied by adding another half knot to the normal square knot.

The button knot

The button knot is an attractive bead-like knot which can give a three-dimensional effect to macramé. Diagram 8 shows how it is tied.

1 Knot one square knot leaving a small space below it
2 Knot at least three square knots
3 Thread the filler cords from front to back as in diagram 8 by bringing them through the space left above them
4 Pull on the filler cords, causing the sinnet to roll up, bring the filler cords down, and secure with another square knot

Alternate square knot cylinder

The alternate square knot pattern can also be made up into a tubular shape. This method of knotting may look complex but is in fact very easy to do. A cylinder requires at least three groups of four cords which can hang either from a circular holding cord or from a straight bar.

When started from a straight bar there will have to be two or three rows of flat alternate square knots worked first before the cylinder can be formed. Label the cords 1–12 and tie square knots with cords 1–4, 5–8 and 9–12; for the next row tie square knots with cords 3–6, 7–10 and 11–2. Continue repeating this pattern, which will form a sock-like tube. Any number of cords can be tied to form a cylinder in this way, making tubes which can be the basis of things as large as shopping bags or garments.

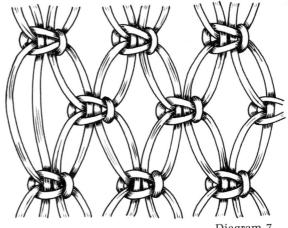

Diagram 7

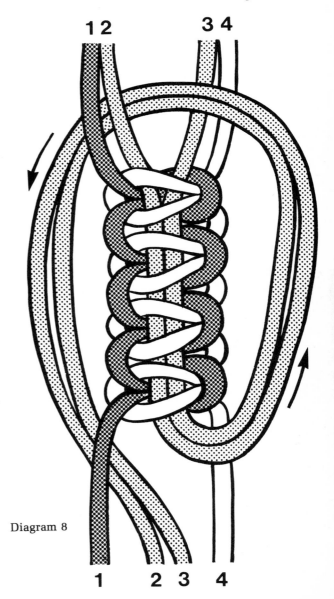

Diagram 8

Cording

Cording is the other important macramé technique and is worked with the half hitch knot. The half hitch is a simple loop made by hitching one cord around another (diagram 9). By itself it does not make a firm knot and will easily unwind unless the cord is hitched a second time to form a double half hitch or, as it is more simply called, a clove hitch. The clove hitch can be worked horizontally (diagram 10), diagonally (diagram 11) or vertically (diagram 12) or it can form an angle (diagram 13). Horizontal and diagonal cording are similar, each cord in turn being knotted over the leader cord. The leader can be one of the set on cords twisted into place and secured with a pin as in diagram 11, or can be a separate cord added to the piece. In vertical cording all the clove hitches are tied with one working cord which has to be much longer than the rest of the cords.

Using these three methods of tying the clove hitch it is virtually possible to control and knot any design you choose. The cloud formation in 'Hunter of the East' (at the top left of the photograph on p. 106 in Chapter 14) was knotted using this technique. Cording is also useful for shaping edges (diagram 13), for making contrasting textural and decorative patterns and forming three-dimensional raised knots as in the berry knot. The clove hitch can also be used for mounting cords onto a foundation cord.

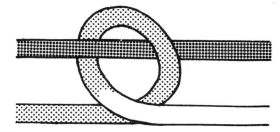

Diagram 9

Diagram 10

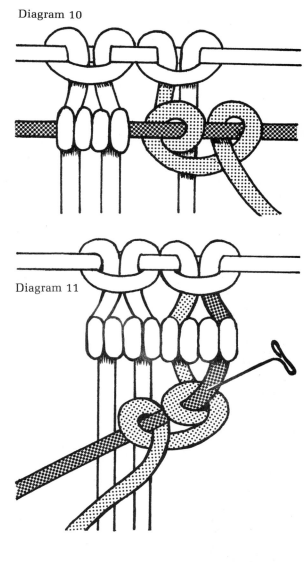

Diagram 11

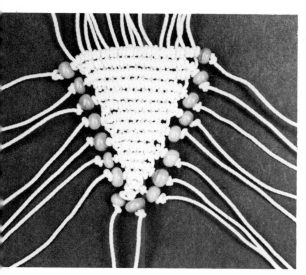

A triangular piece of horizontal cording, the ends finished with a bead and an overhand knot

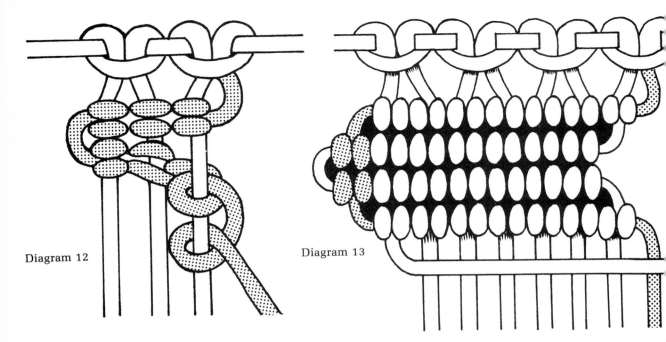

Diagram 12

Diagram 13

A piece of cording showing how this type of knot can be used to make a figurative design. The design is drawn onto a piece of tracing paper which is pinned onto the working board beneath the knotting and acts as its guideline

This African mask made of clay and fired using raku techniques has a head-dress of jute, glass beads, vegetable ivory beads and hand-made ceramic crescent shapes

The girl wears a multi-colour leather waistcoat laced together with Chinese crown knots. The dog is held by a leather leash also worked in Chinese crown knots. The horse wears a decorative fly fringe; the fringe and leading rope are both knotted in soft cotton

This necklace is knotted in macramé twine and decorate with glass beads and shells

Wrap Knots and Tassels

A popular method of finishing a piece of macramé is to gather the loose ends together and to form a tassel with them using a wrap knot. The wrap knot is also a useful knot to incorporate into the body of a piece of macramé. For this knot you will require a darning needle which should be threaded onto the length of cord required for the knot before you start, as it is very difficult to hold the knot firmly in place and thread a needle at the same time. Follow diagram 14 and pull the cord through at the end pulling the top loops into the middle of the wrap. Cut the end of the cord to the same length as the rest of the tassel.

A variation of this tassel that you might like to try is the snaked whipping (diagram 15) where a decorative finish is sewn into the wrap knot using a darning needle.

The berry tassel (diagram 16) has a small wrap top and bottom. The ball of the tassel is knotted in vertical clove hitches on cords from the centre core. With each row an increased number of cords are used until the widest point is reached; then the number of cords are decreased.

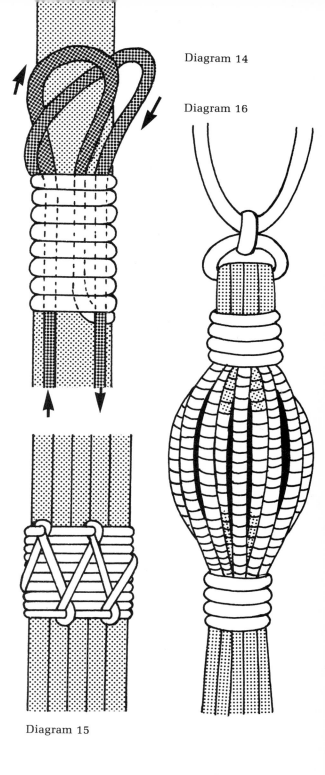

Diagram 14

Diagram 16

Diagram 15

Berry tassels, snaked whipping and wrap knots form the decoration on this little hanging

Decorative Knots

The berry knot

The berry knot combines both cording and
square knots worked over multiples of eight
cords. It starts and finishes with two flat
knots. The central blackberry pattern is
worked in diagonal cording using one set of
four cords as leaders and the others as
working cords. To create a three-
dimensional effect push the back of the
corded area forward to form a dome
(diagrams 17a and b).

The Chinese crown knot

This knot shown in six stages in diagram 18
can be used either as a decorative knot or as
a sinnet where it forms a heavy, strong and
slightly elastic cord. It can be worked with
two or four cords or multiples of these.

Lovers' knot

The lovers' knot is formed by intertwining
two overhand knots together as in
diagram 19.

A turk's head knot flattened out

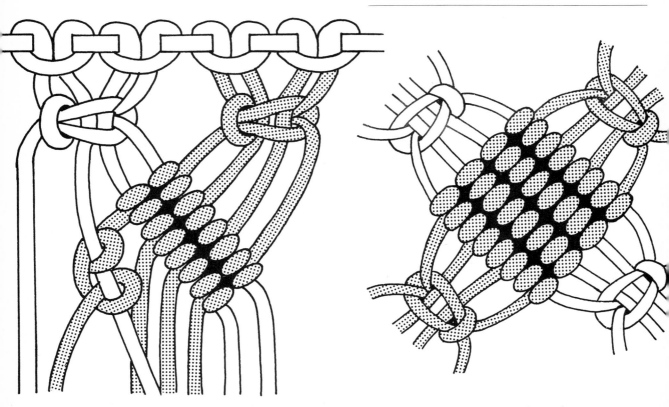

Diagram 17(a) **The start of a berry knot**

Diagram 17(b) **A complete berry knot**

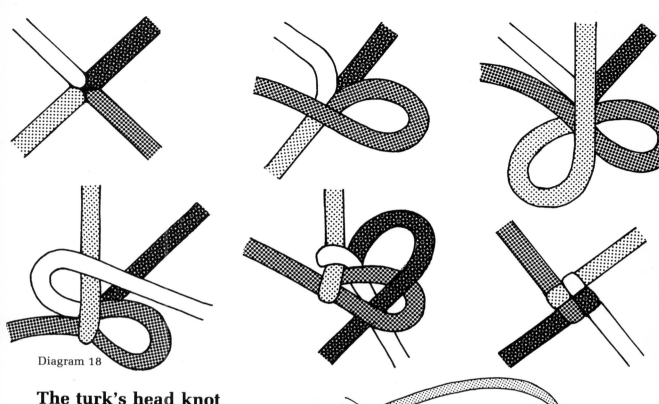

Diagram 18

The turk's head knot

This knot (diagrams 20(a) and (b) and 21) is a tubular knot which is usually worked around a cylindrical object. Diagrams 20(a) and (b) show a single knot which can be duplicated again and again (diagram 21) until the tube is large enough for your purposes. The single knot can be flattened out to form a decorative knot suitable for braids, as in the photograph on p. 70.

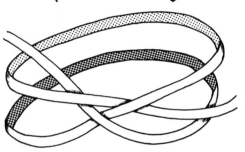

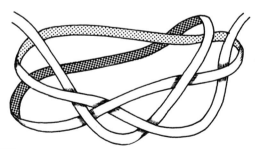

Diagram 20(a) and (b)

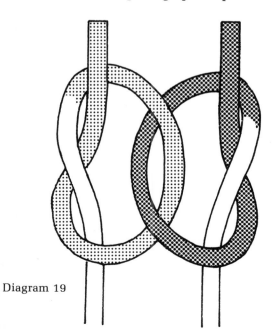

Diagram 19

Diagram 21

27

Working in the Round

Most macramé is worked flat on a working
board but occasionally it becomes necessary
to knot an article in the round. The alternate
square knot cylinder describes one way of
doing this and there are two other ways of
using this method that alleviate the need for
stitched seams. In one case the cords start at
the centre and are worked outwards to form
a flat circular article like a table mat
(diagram 22) and the second case combines
both the other methods. The cords start at
the centre and then become tubular in shape
like skull caps and other types of hat.
When working tubular shapes the cords are
set onto a circular foundation cord and the
work progresses downwards in the normal
way, so a working board is no longer
suitable and a three-dimensional working
surface is needed (diagram 23). This will
have to be as closely related to the size of
the article as possible. Many different
domestic items, padded to take pins, can be
used for this, including upturned
wastepaper baskets, pudding basins and
polystyrene wig blocks.

**The back of a skull cap showing both circular
and tubular knotting**

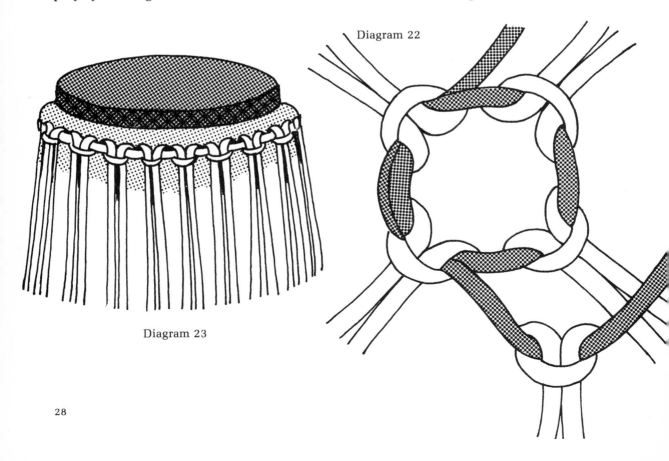

Diagram 22

Diagram 23

28

Colour

The colours of the cords and the ways in which these colours can be related to the work have also to be considered. The simplest way of injecting interesting colours and textures into a piece of macramé is to mix cords of different colours and fibres together in a single article. An example of this is the tunic, 'Beachcomber', which combines cords of brown and pink linen, white silk, coffee cotton and natural jute to give an unusual surface finish to the garment.

When bands of cords of different colours have been attached to their supporting foundation cord or dowel they can be manipulated in various ways to obtain different colour combinations. The coloured cords can be moved out of their original alignment by concealing them in leader cords in rows of clove hitches, or by interchanging working and filler cords to either hide or display a contrasting shade. Extra colour can be obtained by simply adding extra cords to the work or can be removed by attaching unwanted cords to the back of the work until they are needed again. There are many exciting, colourful cords available today, especially in synthetics, and these give a good deal of scope for experiment.

Different colours knotted through each other can be seen in this section of a wall hanging

A close-up of a part of a tunic knotted in a variety of different cords and colours. Natural jute, white silk, brown and pink linen and coffee coloured cotton were used

4 Working in Leather

Leather is a versatile and spectacular material which can be soft and supple or as rigid as a piece of wood. Its qualities enable it to be sewn, knotted, carved, stretched, compressed and laminated, and because of these various properties it is an excellent material for using in macramé. When cut into strips of thonging it is useful for tying knots both in sinnets and in larger areas, thus adding more tactile and textural finishes to your repertoire of macramé designs.

Types of Leather and Tools

There are a number of different types of leather that can be used in macramé. Thonging can be made of rawhide, goatskin, calf or suede and you can also buy suede splits which have a suede face on each side of the thong. Thicker leathers (ox, cow, or calf hides) like those used in the manufacture of boots can be used as a foundation for thinner leather thonging. A simple example of this would be a decorative thonging sinnet supported and fastened along the length of a heavy leather belt. A heavy piece of leather could also be carved, pierced and painted for use as an integral part of a necklace or a wall hanging.

There are not many tools required in the cutting and preparation of leather for macramé work. You will need a metal rule, a medium and a small knife, a pair of

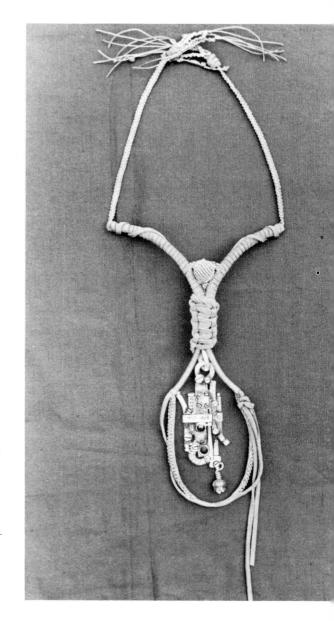

A silver and garnet pendant, designed and executed by Michael Bolton, is incorporated into a suede and twine necklace. The thonging is made of suede splits in dark red which exactly matches the colour of the fishing twine

scissors, a revolving punch or two hand punches of different sizes and an awl for making stitching holes. Leather should be sewn with a waxed thread. Unwaxed thread can be used providing it has first been drawn across a piece of beeswax. Thin suedes, however, can be stitched together using a sewing machine.

Knotting with Thonging

You should use leather thonging for tying knots and although this material may seem stiff to handle at first, it can be quite easily and creatively worked into many varieties of knotting patterns.

A disadvantage of using leather is that the animal hides are limited in length, and ways must be found to obtain thonging long enough to knot more ambitious projects. The easiest way to obtain long lengths of thonging is to buy it in rolls which have already been joined together. These rolls come in lengths of 50m (55yd) or more, but bought thonging is expensive. A cheaper way of obtaining thongs is to make your own by cutting them from a piece of leather.

One method of making thonging is to cut a piece of leather into narrow strips using a metal rule, preferably a safety one with a groove for the fingers running along the top, and a sharp handyman's knife. For very thin leather you could use a pair of household scissors or a surgeon's scalpel.

Each end of every strip of leather should be pared. To pare a piece of leather the skin should be supported upon a hard, flat surface like a piece of marble. To avoid cutting yourself (if the knife should slip) the hand holding the leather should be positioned behind the knife, which is held at an angle to the work. Push the knife away from you, cutting off a thin layer of skin and repeat until the end of the thong is only half its original thickness. The ends can then be glued together to form a long strip. A 'wet' glue can be used such as Dryad's vegetable glue or the American Elmer's Sobo rubber cement. Wet glues should be used when the join does not receive a great deal of wear and tear as most such glues are not waterproof. For harder wear use a contact

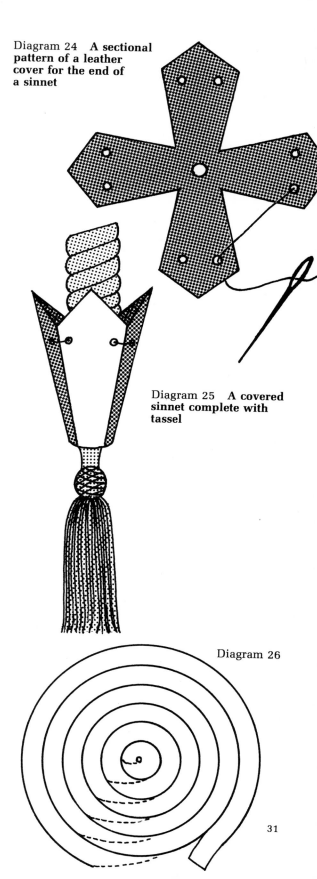

Diagram 24　**A sectional pattern of a leather cover for the end of a sinnet**

Diagram 25　**A covered sinnet complete with tassel**

Diagram 26

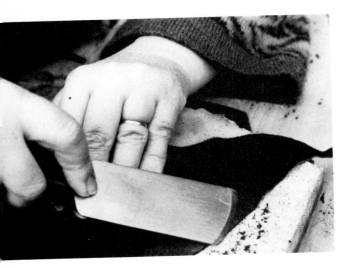

glue like the English Evo-Stik or American Weldwood, which is spread on each piece to be joined and allowed to become tacky before the edges are pressed together.

Thonging can also be cut into long lengths by drawing a series of equidistant circles with a compass from a centre point onto a piece of leather (see diagram 26). Cut along the line of the circles making a cross cut into every subsequent circle. It will be necessary to wet and stretch the leather afterwards to make it lie flat.

The best type of thonging to use for knotting is rawhide, which is strong enough to be knotted when it is damp, thus making tighter knots. Care should be taken when using other types of thonging that you do not pull the knots too tightly or the thong will snap.

Laminated Leather

Leather is only as thick as its origional hide but it is possible to make larger and thicker three-dimensional pieces of leather, suitable for macramé decorations, by lamination. Any odd scraps and thicknesses of leather can be used. Roughen the surfaces of the scraps and join them one on top of the other using a contact glue as an adhesive. Imaginative shapes can be built up this way by leaving projecting pieces of different coloured leathers outside the main body of the laminated block. When the glue is dry the block can then be carved to show the marbled effect of the different coloured layers. Small holes can be punched into the block to enable it to be threaded into the macramé.

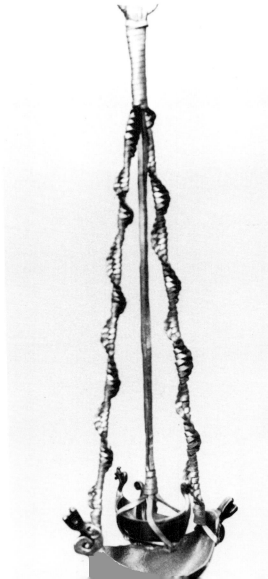

Top left:
This photograph shows the position of the hands and knife during paring

Left:
'Viking ships' features minute pewter dishes suspended from half hitch sinnets knotted with silver leather thongs

Right:
This leather mobile, 'Brønnoysund', is knotted in two thicknesses of thonging. Square knots, cording and wrapping techniques have been used

Above:
A leather cape could have a thong decoration on a wide hemline. Some of the cords are still attached to the body of the cape

Above:
A laminated leather knob hanging at the bottom of 'Brønnoysund'

5 Clay and Ceramic Techniques

If you look at an exhibition of macramé work the decorations, hanging pots, lamp bases, chimes and so on, which are integral parts of many macramé projects, are often made of pottery. The ability to design and make original ceramic items for incorporating into a piece of macramé must give the craft potter a slight advantage over other macramé workers, but only a slight one, for there is now a vast range of different types of pottery which can be bought over the shop counter. Most craft potters will also be pleased to design and make suitable pieces of pottery for you, or alternatively copy your own design. It would be impossible in just one chapter to cover every aspect of both ceramic techniques and of all the different types of pottery that can be both bought and made, so I have chosen a few simple methods of making ceramics that can be used with macramé and described the different types of clay and firing techniques that are used in pottery.

Types of Clay and Firing Techniques

Earthenware and terracotta

The majority of bought and handmade pottery is made of earthenware. Earthenware clay is coloured white or off-white and terracotta clay is brown in colour and when fired changes to brick red. Pottery is fired in a kiln twice. The first firing, known as the

A slab-built stoneware lampbase. The macramé shade repeats its shape. Both base and shade have a sun motif on the front

biscuit firing, is heated to a low temperature (about 1000°C) to make the clay porous and able to absorb the liquid glaze which is applied before the second or glost firing. Earthenware Pottery is fired at a lower temperature than stoneware and because of this a far greater range of coloured glazes are available for decorating the surface of the pottery. Care should be taken here for some colours are extremely bright and unless discretion is used the results could be so garish as to be quite unsuitable for use with macramé.

The craft potter sometimes has difficulty in making the glaze fit the clay body, with the resulting crazing of the glaze. Watch for this when making hanging vases and plant pots as crazed vessels will not hold water and could ruin a hanging. Factory-produced articles do not, as a rule, have this flaw.

Stoneware

Stoneware requires a high-firing clay. It differs from earthenware in the fact that its glost firing rises to a very high temperature of 1250°C. This makes the clay body extremely hard and impervious to water and the result is a tough, waterproof piece of pottery. A tabletop made in stoneware and suspended from a macramé hanging would be able to stand a great deal of wear and tear. The glaze colours of stoneware are more subtle than the earthenware ones and combine satisfactorily with macramé knotting.

Porcelain

While stoneware is the thickest type of pottery, porcelain is the thinnest. Good examples of porcelain should be translucent. Porcelain clay is the most difficult clay to work with because as it dries it becomes brittle. Some potters even fire their pieces before they finish the fine details on a model and then work on the biscuited piece. Porcelain beads and ornaments can look most attractive in a wall hanging and the ideal position for a factory-made translucent porcelain bowl would be to suspend it in a macramé hanging in front of a window.

A slab-built bell with African-type decorations on its front and sides. The bell pull is worked in cording and the bell has a variety of sinnets and wooden beads knotted into its top

Raku

This is one of the most decorative and original types of pottery that it is possible to make. As it is fired outdoors, in a homemade firebrick kiln using wood, coke or propane gas as fuel, a raku firing is generally a class or group project. Raku is made with a clay that has a coarse, open body to enable it to withstand the sudden thermal shock that it receives when the piece is plunged into the hot kiln. A raku pot is first given a biscuit firing, glazed and placed into a red hot kiln with a pair of long tongs and left there for upwards of half an hour until the glaze becomes liquified. It is then removed and smothered in sawdust or grass to prevent air getting to the pot and then the pot is quenched in a bucket of water.

The results can be fantastic: green copper glazes become shiny copper lustres, some areas of glaze run and intermingle forming stalagmite-like effects on the edges of pots

Above:
A group of raku pottery. An African mask has holes for cords pierced on the top of its head, the sides of its face and on its chin. The raku pot made by the coiling method is for a plant hanging. The large blue and black bead in the foreground will be used in a hanging table

Right:
Stoneware, earthenware and porcelain pottery. The broken porcelain figure will not be wasted. The broken edges have holes for cords pierced all around them. The bell can be seen complete with its macramé bell pull, decorations and hanging (on the previous page). The earthenware dish has three holes for its hanging punched through it

and colours such as persian blue seem to have an added richness. As the firing temperature does at no time rise above 1000°C the piece remains porous and a plant could be put directly into a raku pot without having to use an inner terracotta plantpot. The macramé hanging in this case should, of course, be made of rot-proof cord.

Cold clay

Cold clay is a manufactured ceramic
material that does not require to be fired. It
is an air-setting clay which sets rock hard
with a smooth marble-like finish. Most
hand-built articles that can be made in
ordinary clay can also be made in cold clay.
When dry the surface of a cold clay article
can be painted with gouache paints and
given a shiny waterproof varnish finish. It is
invaluable to the macramé worker for
making small ornamental plaques for
hangings, beads and other small items.

Hand-built Methods

Naturally the craft potter with throwing
ability can make all manner of pots and
dishes suitable for use with macramé, but
pottery made by hand-built methods can
also be used and will blend most
successfully with a knotted object. Here are
the hand-built methods that I have used for
making the ceramic tabletop project in
Chapter 10 and for the hanging pot and
saucer projects from Chapter 9.

A group of bought pottery. The ginger jar would
be suitable to use with the 'Geisha' plant
hanging (see Chapter 12). The small tureen and
the egg coddler both have handles that will take
fairly large macramé sinnets. A wardrobe
hanging could support two or three pomanders
like the one shown here in the foreground

Coil pot

A pot like the one shown in the 'Geisha'
project, (p. 91, Chapter 12), can be made by
the method of coiling.

MATERIALS

**A number of long smooth coils of clay not
more than 2cm (¾in) in diameter**

A whirler

**A small batt – a tile or board on which the
pot may be placed**

METHOD

1 Starting at the base of the pot make a flat,
   circular shape about 5cm (2in) in diameter
   from a piece of rolled out clay. Place it
   upon the batt which is centred upon
   the whirler.

2 Spiral the first coil onto the top of the outer edge of the base and press firmly into it (diagram 27). The whirler will enable you to turn the pot as you go. Continue working the coil in a spiral around the base and upwards until all the coil has been used up.

3 Add more coils, one at a time, continuing to work upwards, smoothing and pinching the edges of the coils into each other both inside and out as you go. Form the shape of the pot by spiralling the coils tighter or looser according to your design (diagram 28) With this type of pot big, swelling curves are best. If the pot shows any sign of sagging leave it for a few hours until it is firmer.

4 Continue building the coils one upon the other until the pot is the size that you require. Do not add any water as you build up the coils; the clay should be damp enough to adhere to itself and all the coils should be firmly welded together, both on the inside and the outside of the pot.

5 This pot can be made in cold clay, earthenware, stoneware or raku. In the case of cold clay it can be painted and waterproofed. Terracotta clay would be suitable to be left just biscuited, and earthenware and stoneware could be wholly or partially glazed.

Slab-built tabletop

Although both come under the heading of hand-built pottery, the tabletop and the saucer are made in a completely different way from the coil pot. These two items are made by a method known as slab building. Slab building is a method of constructing pottery by rolling out slabs of clay and bending or joining these slabs together to form the shape of the ceramic. The tabletop is a very easy piece of pottery to make as it is the simplest form of slab construction.

MATERIALS

A piece of sacking or stiff canvas about 60cm (2ft) square

A rolling pin

A pair of wooden strips on which the rolling pin runs to give an even thickness of clay

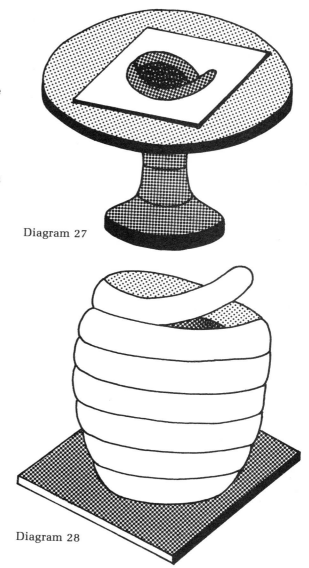

Diagram 27

Diagram 28

A small tool for piercing holes

A lump of soft prepared clay

METHOD

1 Flatten the clay with the hand onto the centre of the piece of sacking.

2 Beginning at the centre and working first in one direction and then in the other, roll out the clay, lifting and separating the clay and the sacking regularly whilst rolling (diagram 29). Prick any air bubbles that appear on the surface of the clay with a pin.

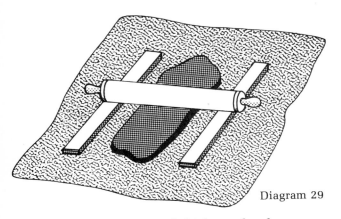

Diagram 29

Right:
Four different tabletops and dishes:

(a) **An earthenware dish painted in stripes of chestnut and black lustre glaze**

(b) **A mottled raku-glazed tabletop**

(c) **A stoneware tabletop decorated with slip (liquid clay) glazes. The daisy pattern is punched out right through the tabletop**

(d) **A terracotta dish with a linocut relief design picked out in black lustre glaze**

3 When the required thickness has been reached — not more than 1.5cm (½in) or less than 6mm (¼in) — trim the edges of the clay to the shape that you require (round, oval, kidney, etc.) with a sharp knife and peel off the sacking. It is much easier to hold the clay slab if you support it along the length of your arm.

4 Place the slab on a flat surface and leave until it is firm. Before the tabletop dries out it is necessary to pierce in it the three holes through which the hanging cords will pass. A metal lipstick case is a useful implement to use as a punch for making these holes and if you think that this makes rather a large hole remember that a group of at least four cords must pass through it, and the shrinkage on a piece of pottery that has been fired is about 1 in 10. Punch the holes equidistant from each other and at least 5cm (2in) in from the edge of the piece.

5 Leave the tabletop until it is bone dry, biscuit and glaze.

Shell-shaped saucer dish

A shell shaped saucer dish can be made in a similar way to the tabletop.

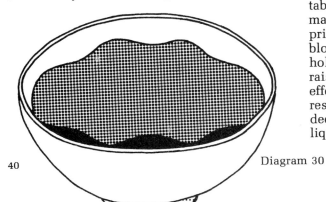

METHOD

1 Roll out a piece of clay and cut it into a circular shape.

2 Place the circular piece of clay into a shallow basin. The basin can be made of any material as it only acts as a support while the clay is drying.

3 The edge of the clay circle will be much greater than that of the basin and will frill around its rim. Arrange these frills evenly around the basin and leave to dry (diagram 30).

4 Remove from the basin and smooth edges where necessary. A pot made in cold clay like this could be waterproofed and used as a mould for a similar saucer in papier mâché.

Lino Relief Decoration

Although there are many ways to decorate these items, there is one method of decoration that is eminently suitable for flat surfaces and could be used to good effect here; this is linocut relief decoration. This method can be simply performed by cutting a linocut design into a block of linoleum and firmly impressing the design into a slab of soft clay before it has been trimmed into a tabletop, dish, etc. Remove immediately, making sure that every part of the block has printed. Remember when designing the lino block that the areas left uncut will form hollows in the clay and the cut areas the raised decoration, a completely opposite effect to that of a printed linocut. The resulting relief design can, when dry, be decorated with coloured slips — coloured liquid clays — before it is glazed.

Diagram 30

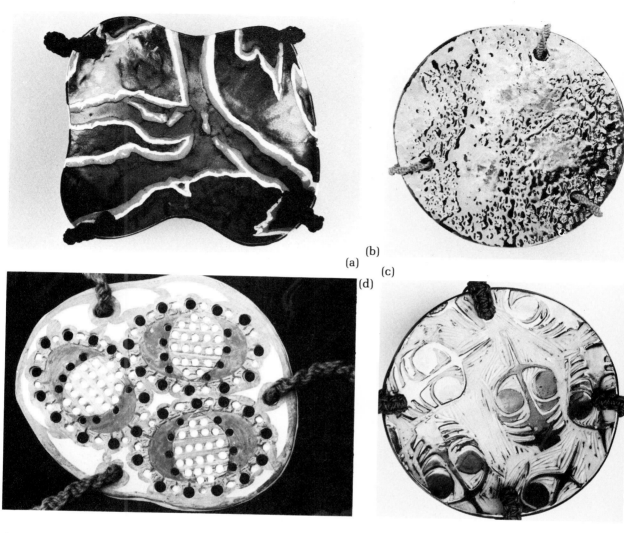

(a)

(b)

(c)

(d)

Some examples of ceramic decorations. All have been pierced with holes of varying sizes

Above:
The linocut design 'Greenhouse' printed on paper

This terracotta tabletop has the linocut design 'Greenhouse' impressed into its surface. Black, white and blue glazes have been painted onto its dark red surface

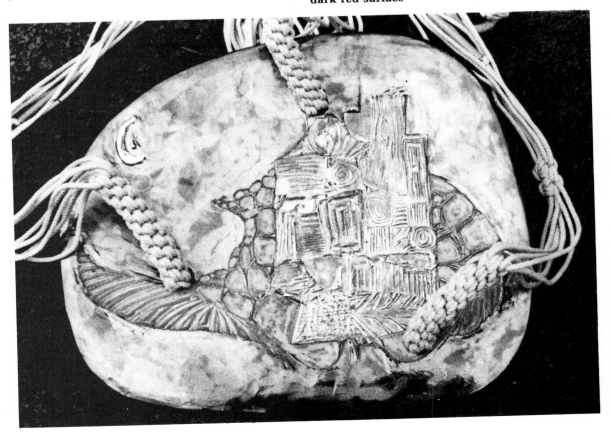

6 Making Papier Mâché

Papier mâché is a plastic craft related to both ceramics and sculpture. As an adjunct to macramé it is invaluable in that it does not require expensive equipment, doesn't break if it is dropped and is extremely lightweight. Paper is the raw material of papier mâché and it is easy to make inexpensive pots, tabletops and dishes by following the simple instructions in this chapter.

There are two different ways of making papier mâché. The most usual is to make the article of overlapping strips of paper glued together with paste and left to harden. The other type of papier mâché can be made by pulping the paper, which is then mixed with various adhesives that render it suitable for many different purposes.

Paper pulp

There are a number of different ways of making paper pulp and you may care to experiment to find the most suitable combination of ingredients for your own projects. Here is one way of making this pulp.

1 Loosely fill a galvanized bucket with torn pieces of paper about 3cm (1¼in) square. The best types of paper to use are newsprint, paper towels or toilet paper. Cover the paper with 1l (2pt) of water and allow to soak for at least 24 hours.

Two macramé and papier mâché pots. The sinnets on the left hand 'Thump' pot are actually glued to the surface of the pot and support it. The shell theme of the shell-shaped dish hanging on the right has been continued with shells glued to the outside of the pot and to the bottom of the fringe. The ring from which it hangs is a fisherman's lead weight

2 Boil the paper in its water until the fibres are loosened, adding more water as it evaporates. This will take upwards of half an hour.

3 Using an electric mixer or blender, preferably one with metal blades, pulp the paper putting only a very little paper into the blender at each mixing. If you have not got a blender use a metal hand whisk, although this will prove to be a long and tedious job.

4 Squeeze as much water as possible out of the pulp and add a few drops of oil of cloves as a preservative. This mixture, with nothing added, is suitable for use in plaster casts and for modelling very small objects.

5 Pulp that gives a smooth surface finish when applied to small and medium sized articles needs the addition to the mixture of 2 tbsp of wallpaper paste, 2 tbsp of ball clay or whiting (to act as a filler), and 1 tbsp of linseed oil (to make the article stronger and waterproof).

6 Large articles like tabletops require the addition of 2 tbsp of liquid glue to the above mixture. Dryad's vegetable glue is a suitable one to use. In America it is possible to buy packets of ready made papier mâché pulp. Strong pulp made with glue and paste should never be used directly on the surface of a plaster mould as it will adhere firmly to it.

Constructing Papier Mâché Shapes

A papier mâché article can be made in two ways. One is to reproduce the existing shape of a pot, dish or other suitable article by using it as a mould, and the other is to model an object using an armature as a support.

Reproducing an existing shape

This is the simplest way of making a pot by papier mâché. The two designs here show how to make a round pot and a saucer dish, both of which could be used with the hanging projects featured in chapter 12.

A balloon pot painted in tan oil paint and decorated with areas of gold leaf. The bracelet is formed of thin card covered with papier mâché strips. The square knot sinnet is glued to the outside and the bead is 'eyed'

Round balloon pot

MATERIALS
1 round balloon
A quantity of torn strips of paper approx. 3×8cm (1¼×3⅛in)
Wallpaper paste

METHOD
1 Blow up a round balloon until it reaches the size that you require for the pot. Stand the balloon upon a cup for ease of working.

2 Cover the entire surface (except the neck) of the balloon with seven overlapping layers of pasted paper strips. First dampen the paper and then apply a liberal amount of paste to it using your fingers. Do not paste the layer of paper next to the balloon. If you use different types of newsprint (e.g. the cartoon page or the yellow or pink pages) it will be easier to see where the layers overlap.

3 Leave it until it is completely dry, puncture the balloon withdraw it from the papier mâché pot.

A saucer dish of papier mâché strips with its edges bound ready for painting

4 Cut a round hole around the neck of the pot with a pair of scissors, large enough to take a plant pot, and bind the edges of the hole with small strips of paper (see diagram 31). Place in an oven and bake completely dry in a temperature of not more than 250°C (480°F). The base of this pot will be rounded; do not make a standing rim for this pot as it will be suspended by a macramé hanging.

Saucer-shaped dish

A china dish will form the mould upon which the papier mâché form is worked. A mould could also be made of varnished and waterproofed cold clay. You can either make a mould of the outside of the dish or of the inside. An interior model will shrink to a size appreciably smaller than its original mould.

MATERIALS

A china dish, shell-shaped or any other decorative, shallow shape

A quantity of torn strips of paper

Wallpaper paste

Petroleum jelly

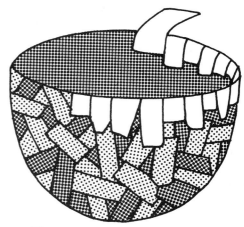

Diagram 31

METHOD

1 Grease the dish mould with a layer of petroleum jelly and cover it with a layer of wet, unpasted paper strips.

2 Cover this wet paper with seven layers of wet, pasted paper exactly as you did for the balloon pot. If a stronger pot is required add more layers of paper.

3 Leave the papier mâché dish until it is firm enough to handle, remove from the mould, trim and bind the edges and gently press out any excess moisture that

45

may remain. Place the paper dish in the oven and gently bake until it is completely dry. Any saucer-shaped dish or bowl can be made in this way providing that there is no undercutting on the surface of its original mould (see diagram 32).

Diagram 32

Creating a new form using an armature

An armature is usually considered to be a support made of bent wire, but in papier mâché it can be anything that adds firmness to the piece. An armature can be made of card, cardboard, wood, thick twists of paper or anything which is firm and suitably shaped for your project. This method differs from the previous one in the fact that, where an existing shape was reproduced, the mould (ie. a balloon or dish) was removed when the papier mâché was dry. When an armature is used it is the skeleton of the piece and remains inside it. Here is a method of making a hanging tabletop for the project in Chapter 10 using a cardboard armature.

A small papier mâché temple supporting a bead curtain is photographed against a collage background. The armatures for this model include cardboard shoe boxes, thin card and dowelling. The finials of the columns are beads

MATERIALS

A piece of thick cardboard or two thinner pieces glued together

A sheet of plastic larger than the cardboard

Approx. 1l (2pt) of strong papier mâché pulp

Wallpaper paste

A quantity of torn paper strips

A board slightly larger than the finished tabletop

METHOD

1 Cut the cardboard to the size required for the tabletop (square, round, free-form and so on) and pierce three holes in it equidistant from each other (see Chapter 5). Keep these holes clear throughout the making of the table.

2 Bind the cut edges of the table with two thicknesses of pasted paper strips and coat the base with another two layers of overlapping pasted strips. Leave to dry.

3 Spread the sheet of plastic over the board, which should be light enough to transport to a warm place when the table is completed. Spread a layer of papier mâché pulp over the sheet and roll it smooth with a rolling pin to a thickness of between 1 and 2cm (⅜ to ¾in).

4 Paste the face of the cardboard tabletop and place it face down onto the pulp. Paste the edges of the table and smooth the pulp evenly up its sides. Remove any excess pulp.

5 Leave it face down to dry under weights to prevent warping. As the tabletop is on a moveable board it can be placed in an unused room near a radiator. It should take between one and three weeks to dry.

6 When it is completely dry fill any irregularities with little pieces of fine pulp. Re-dry and sandpaper away any rough edges.

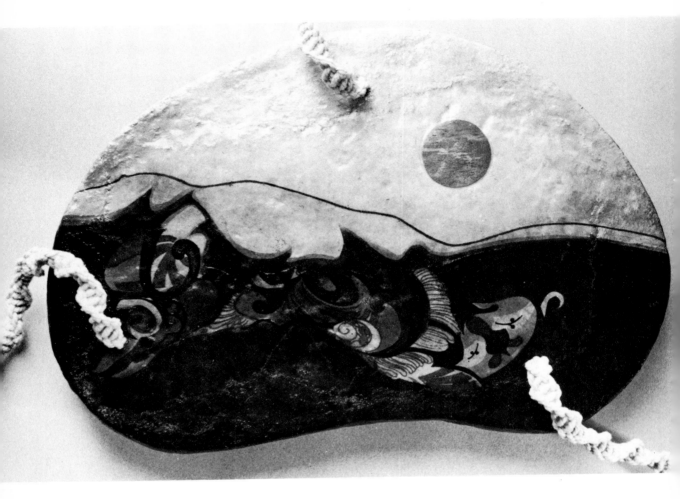

Decoration and Finishes

Before the surface of a piece of papier mâché can be decorated it must first be sealed. Suitable materials for sealing the surface of a piece include water-based wall paint, lacquer and varnish. For a really fine, smooth surface rub down and cover the article with several thick coats of gesso, which is a material made of whitening and glue and can be obtained in most fine art shops.

For a rich textured finish small pieces of lace, crochet, tatting or other decorative materials, including macramé, can be pasted or glued to the outside of a pot, covered with a layer of water-based paint and the decoration highlighted by rubbing the surface with a mixture of varnish and contrasting coloured oil paint.

The surface of the tabletop. The design is an etching which has been glued onto the pulp surface. The rim has been painted to match the print

Photographs, prints, etchings and any other pictures except watercolours can be moistened and pasted or glued to the surface of a papier mâché item. Decorative wrapping is also suitable for this type of embellishment. You can also paint your own designs onto the surface of a piece of papier mâché; this is the method used in the finest examples of this craft. The best surface to work on is the one made with gesso.

Paper pulp also lends itself to the technique of incising. The wet pulp is spread over the surface of a papier mâché article and the surface teased and punched with a tool,

'Hampton Court', a wall hanging worked in many shades of blue and green

The table hanging in the conservatory of St Julian's, Sevenoaks, combines white cord and a subtle dolomite glaze on the surface of the ceramic tabletop

A group of plant hangings includes containers made of ceramics, papier mâché and shells

A hanging table made with a papier mâché tabletop

piece of dowelling, a hairpin or any other blunt instrument. Keep the tool moistened to prevent it adhering to the mash.

Most clear varnishes are suitable for the finishing coat over a papier mâché article. Both gloss and matt varnishes are easily obtainable but some matt varnishes do give a slightly yellowish tinge to the piece. Today there are a number of finishes that can be applied to papier mâché to render it waterproof and suitable for use outdoors. Paints that contain acrylic resins, epoxy resins and polyurethenes are all suitable for waterproofing. If fibreglass resin and a catalyst are used the piece would even stand washing with hot water and detergents.

This close-up of the 'Thump' pot shows its surface decorated with tatting and lace

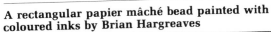

A rectangular papier mâché bead painted with coloured inks by Brian Hargreaves

The knot used on the side of the 'Thump' pot is based on the design of the thump mat used by sailors to protect the deck from being battered by deck blocks

7 Serendipity

The dictionary defines serendipity as the faculty of making happy and unexpected discoveries by accident. Perhaps 'accident' is not *quite* the right word to use here, for the discoveries that we hope to make are intentionally sought for the purpose of combining them with macramé. It is the object of this chapter to give you some idea of where you can find just the right item to complete your work, and that will also add to its æsthetic or utilitarian value.

Objets Trouvés

It was the Surrealists in the early twentieth century who urged the intrinsic worth of the found object. They considered that the found object is one, when viewed amongst a number of other objects, that stimulated the mind into visualizing it in another context to the one in which it was originally conceived. When a natural or ready-made object is combined with various other items related to each other only by the artist's powers of invention, it becomes divorced from its original purpose and becomes part of an integrated article that was conceived by thought alone.

The ready-made object

This is a term used for an industrially produced man-made article whose original function is altered when the object is used, either by itself or combined with other things, in a creative, artistic context. It is

The bottom of a hanging is wrapped around pieces of grey sheep's fleece

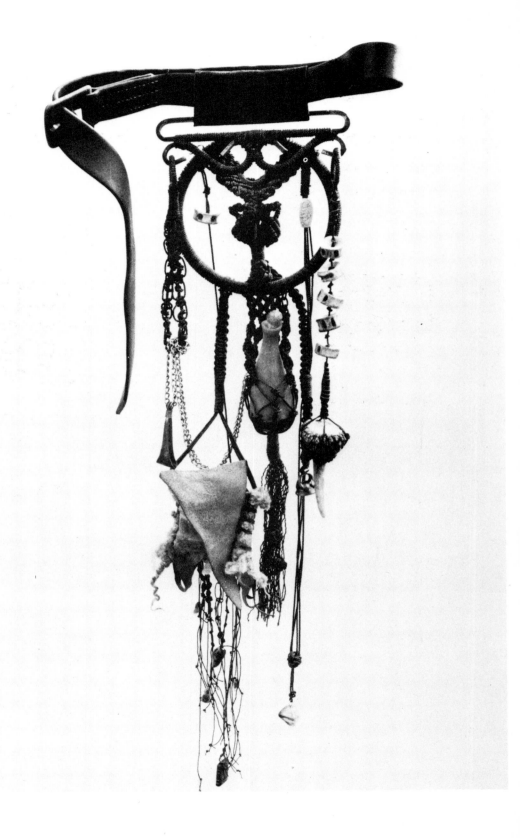

when the ready-made object is combined with macramé, that it is of use to us.

In most homes there are a number of articles, rarely used and easily spared, which could be incorporated into a macramé hanging or sculpture. The garden shed may contain a variety of rusty wheels, pieces of old stove or grate, interestingly shaped, with a hole through them, which would blend suitably into a hanging. It is not necessary to clean away the rust as this can show a pleasing patina and colour. Just clean the area that lies under the macramé cords and give the cleaned area a coat of varnish to prevent it rusting again. Interesting pieces of metal and chain can sometimes be obtained from friends (particularly those who mend their own vehicles) and can also be found thrown away on waste ground.

Objects found indoors include such things as wooden spoons, wooden and china serviette rings, old keys, horsebrasses and mirrors. Providing that the object can be safely attached to the macramé you can use almost any manufactured article. In most cases it is better to harmonize the object with the theme of the hanging, e.g. a wooden spoon would be a suitable item to include in a hanging with a cookery theme. However, it is possible with the disparate collection of items in this group to achieve more startling effects. If you were to knot side by side a number of cords of a strong orange colour and some of shocking pink, the effect would be electric and impart a great vitality to the work. It is possible to knot two or more objects into a hanging that are so different to one another in type, shape and texture that a dramatic effect is obtained, and the observer's attention is held in the same way as when he or she looks at the stimulating colour scheme of pink and orange. The wooden serviette ring and the metal cow bell in 'Buffalo Bell' (Chapter 12) show one example of combining dissimilar objects in this way.

'The Mage's Chatelain', a theatrical prop which has a Kenyan snuff bottle, a nineteenth-century carnelian seal and an amethyst pendulum amongst its hangings

The outside of this papier mâché pot is covered with orange and yellow shells picked up from the beach

The natural object

Drama is not usually invoked when natural objects are added to a piece of macramé. Natural objects are too quiet and subtle in mood and colour for bold, vibrant work.

The best collecting ground for natural objects trouvés is the sea shore. Here the observant collector should be able to find, in the course of an afternoon's casual hunting on the beach, between 20 or 30 pebbles with holes through them. These pebbles could then be easily threaded into a piece of macramé in the place of beads. Other useful items include well-washed bones of seabirds, holed shells, pieces of rope, some already knotted which have been swept

overboard from a fishing vessel, strange gnarled pieces of driftwood and lumps of cork.

The countryside too can prove a very fruitful area, and look here for pieces of wood wrought in unusual shapes, large seed pods, feathers and pieces of sheep's fleece that have been rubbed off onto barbed wire fences. Collecting natural objects for use with macramé is not only inexpensive but it also makes a good excuse, if one is needed, for spending a day at the sea or in the country.

Charity Shops and Bazaars

In nearly every large town there is a shop where second-hand articles are sold in order to obtain money for charity. These and white elephant stalls at Church or school bazaars are good places to look for objects with which to embellish a piece of macramé. Jewellery is worth inspecting. Bead necklaces can be a most economical source of beads, but make sure that the holes through them are large enough for your requirements. Enamelled plaques from broken earrings, small decorative brooches and odd balls of wool can all be useful and worth adding to your stock of macramé materials.

Probably the most useful item that you can buy here are the strong, stiff plastic bracelets that have now gone out of fashion. These can make excellent rings for plant hangings and can always be wrapped or knotted over in cord if they are the wrong colour.

Left:
'For the Spirit of the Place', a hanging that has a number of objets trouvés incorporated into it. The hanging is supported by a branch of a tree. The large section, knotted in silk, linen, leather and wool, has as a centrepiece a rusty piece of iron encrusted with pebbles. The smaller section has as its centrepiece a silver and opal pendant by Michael Bolton. Feathers and fleece are also included

Right:
This brass pot hung by a suede plant-hanging came from Norway. The wood and pewter bowl was also bought in Norway and would make a decorative focal point of another hanging

Craftwork from Other Countries

There are a number of shops nowadays that sell craftwork from one or many different countries, and from these shops it is possible to obtain a great variety of fascinating objects. The Japanese shops offer porcelain pots, dishes and a selection of chimes. From India come figures and decorations of papier mâché, tassels, seed beads and bells. Chinese shops sell dragon and cloisonné beads and ivory discs, but the shops that sell the most suitable articles for use with macramé are the African craft shops. It may be that the simple, unaffected objects that can be bought in these shops blend easily with knotting, which is after all basically an unsophisticated craft. Fibres like jute and linen combine naturally with African masks, ivory snuff bottles and fishbone beads. A look round these shops can soon stimulate your imagination again when you don't know how to complete your knotting.

When you go abroad on holiday remember to keep some spending money aside in case you see any interesting items to add to your macramé collection. It is always useful to keep a number of different objects trouvés, ethnic and second-hand objects in stock as when you are designing a hanging, accessory or piece of jewellery it is useful to have a variety of different objects that you can place against the work in progress in order to see which piece fits in most satisfactorily.

'Sea Shanty'. The finished hanging is worked in American cotton, dish-cloth cotton, twine and decorative wool. The serendipity includes bleached bone, pebbles and an Indian bell

8 Beads

A bead, by a broad definition, is any small decorative object with a hole through it. Beads were probably first used when primitive men and women discovered that shells, teeth and seeds were easy to pierce and string together. In about 3000 B.C. beads made of amethyst, carnelian and garnet were pierced, ground and polished to a very high standard and in many places throughout the world the bead was one of the elements of barter. Lapis lazuli beads probably came as barter beads to pre-dynastic Egypt, Egyptian beads have been found in Celtic burial chambers and the West African trade beads clearly show a Venetian origin in their mosaic designs.

Beads have also played their part in the symbolism of many of the world's religions. In the East strings of beads are used as touch pieces or worry beads and act as a guide to the number of prayers spoken. The Christian rosary is used in much the same way, and can be very elaborate, with beads of precious and semi-precious stones. It can also be so simple that beads are no longer strung on the cords and the prayers are recorded by a series of knots.

This brings us right back again to macramé, where beads are the commonest form of decoration. They can add a focal point, a touch of colour, create a mood or cover an exchange of cords on almost any item from garments to plant hangings. The type of bead selected will depend mainly on the use of the article on which it is to be threaded. For example, a bead of cold clay would not

'Bayaka' is decorated with glass, plastic and gold lustre earthenware beads. The slices of nut are the fruit of the Doom palm and are known as vegetable ivory

57

(a)

(b)

(c)

(d)

Top left:

Glass and china beads:

(a) foil, 'eyed' and combed beads

(b) Venetian Millifiori beads, an African trade bead and a surface decorated glass bead

(c) Oriental dragon, striped silk and opaque beads

(d) Pendant glass beads

Left:

Beads from natural sources:

(a) shells, sections of shell and mother of pearl beads

(b) carved, painted and inlaid wooden beads and a bamboo bead

(c) pebbles, semi-precious stones and carved stone beads

(d) seeds, seed pods, carved bone and ivory and fish vertebrae beads

Above:

Handmade beads:

(a) raku, earthenware and terracotta beads

(b) stoneware and porcelain beads

(c) beads and decorations made in cold clay

(d) papier mâché and paper beads

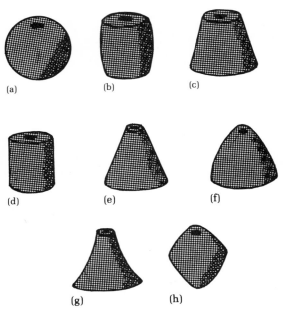

Diagram 33   (a) globular (b) barrel
(c) pear-shaped (d) cylindrical (e) cone-shaped
(f) convex cone (g) concave cone (h) bicone

be suitable for a garment that needs even occasional washing; those made of china, plastic or glass should be used. Size, shape and weight must also be considered in relation to the piece of macramé. Beaded curtains would require lightweight beads while rich, decorative beads could be used in jewellery designs. The most usual shapes of bead are globular, oval, pear-shaped, cylindrical, barrel and cone-shaped. Variations on the cone include the concave and the convex cones, and the bicone (diagram 33).

Types of Bead

China and glass beads

These can be bought from many shops and the range is enormous. As can be seen from the photograph on page 58 they vary from the highly intricate Millifiori Venetian glass beads to simple globular china ones. It is important to ensure that the threading holes in these beads are large enough for the cords to pass through as these holes are extremely difficult to enlarge.

Above:
A section of 'Hunter of the East' showing beads made of fish vertebrae, porcelain, glass and carved ivory

Right:
A necklace of waxed nylon thread embellished with natural decorations. Slices of shell, shells, semi-precious stones, bone and seed pods are intermingled with plain wooden beads

Plastic beads

Plastic beads are easily obtainable in a great variety of colours. They are inexpensive and suitable for most articles that need washing, but they have a dead quality when compared to beads that are made of china or glass and because of this should be used sparingly.

Wooden beads

Unless you have a turning lathe it is better to buy wooden beads rather than trying to carve your own. Wooden beads can be painted, carved, poker-worked, have metal inlays, be square, globular, barrel-shaped and many more. In fact there are nearly as many types of wooden beads as there are one made of glass, but they are lightweight Large numbers of them can be threaded onto a garment like a poncho and it will still not be too heavy to wear.

Beads from natural materials

Primitive cultures still use beads of this type, and it is easy to see a reaction against our sophisticated environment in the attraction that these natural ornaments have for some of us. The sea shore is an area where many natural beads can be found; small holed pebbles are ready to thread and even some shells are pierced. However, it is not difficult to make holes in shells, seed pods, seeds or decorative pieces of bone. The vertebrae of some larger fish also make very attractive beads and it is now possible to buy slices of shell, cut with a power tool, which show their subtle and decorative structure.

Making Ceramic, Cold Clay, Papier Mâché and Paper Beads

Ceramic and papier mâché beads are some of the simplest objects for a craft worker to make. They can be almost any size from extremely large beads the size of a tennis ball down to beads of approximately 2cm (¾in) in diameter. It would be difficult and fiddly for an artist, unless he or she is a specialist in the making of small sculptures, to make a good quality bead smaller than this, and it seems a rather pointless exercise to do so when there are so many other types of small bead readily available. But large beads are usually expensive and unusual shapes are hard to find, so it is better to concentrate on making these types of bead yourself. The easiest way to make a bead is just to mould the material (either clay, cold

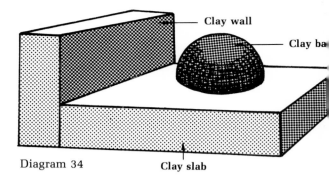

Diagram 34

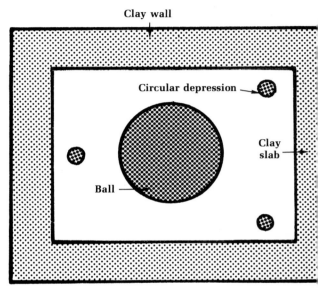

Diagram 35

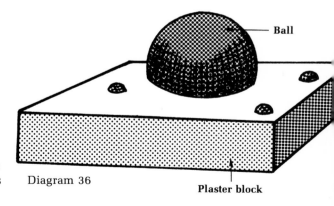

Diagram 36

clay or papier mâché) into a simple shape around a knitting needle which is removed just before the material hardens.

Press moulding

There are a number of ways of making professional looking beads using quite straightfoward techniques. The one described here is press moulding, and it is possible to make a large number of beads exactly the same size as each other by this method using both clay and papier mâché. The instructions are for making a globular bead but many other simple shapes can also be made this way.

MATERIALS

A rubber ball, tennis-ball size or less

Small quantity of clay of a throwing consistency

1kg (2.2lb) fine plaster of paris

1 dessertspoonful green soft soap

METHOD

1 Put the ball exactly halfway into a bed of soft clay (diagram 34). Balls usually have a slight mould mark around them which will assist you to visually divide the ball in half. Make sure that the clay is smooth and tight against the ball.

2 Build a clay wall slightly higher than the ball around the clay bed.

3 Make three small circular depressions around the ball; these will act as keys for the finished cast (diagram 35).

4 Mix sufficient quantity of plaster of paris to fill the area inside the wall. To mix plaster of paris pour approximately 200ml (7fl. oz) cold water into a plastic bowl and sprinkle onto its surface 500g (1.1lb) of fine quality plaster of paris. (Always add plaster to water and not water to plaster.) Stir the mixture with the hand to remove lumps taking care not to make bubbles in the mixture, and when the plaster thickens to the consistency of double cream it is ready to use. Pour the plaster into the cavity, making sure that the surrounding wall and inner block of clay are securely joined together, or else plaster will run everywhere. The top of

the ball should be covered by a layer of plaster at least 2.5cm (1in) thick.

5 When the plaster has hardened peel off the clay wall, turn over the plaster block and remove all the rest of the clay, ensuring that the ball remains in place. You should then have half a ball showing above the plaster block, surrounded by three raised half circles (diagram 36).

6 Rebuild the wall around the plaster block.

7 Mix a solution of of 1 dessertspoonful of green soft soap to 1 cupful of hot water and give the plaster surface, but not the ball, three coats of soapy solution until its surface is slippery.

8 Mix another measure of plaster of paris and repeat stage 4.

9 When the plaster has hardened and the clay wall is removed the two plaster half-moulds can be gently parted and the ball removed. Leave the mould to dry out completely.

For clay

Fill the inside of each half-ball with soft clay. Brush some liquid clay onto both surface edges of the clay to make them adhere to each other and press the two halves of the mould together. (If the ball is larger than 2.5cm (1in) in diameter leave the centre of the ball hollow.) Open the mould, remove the bead, smooth down the join and make its threading hole.

When dry the clay bead can be biscuited and glazed. It is possible to string clay beads onto a nickel-chrome wire in the kiln for earthenware glost firing. Care should be taken that the beads do not touch each other as the wire bends a little in the heat. Make sure also that the wire is trapped securely at both ends. Stoneware beads cannot be fired in this way and the beads will not be able to be glazed all over as they will have to stand directly on the kiln shelf.

For papier mâché

Brush a thin layer of petroleum jelly on the surface of the mould and press papier mâché pulp made with only paper and water into both halves of the ball until both cavities are full and level. Leave until dry. Remove both halves from their moulds and glue them together. Sandpaper away any rough edges and make the threading holes. Identical decorations can be made on each bead by carving a design into the surface of the plaster ball.

Paper beads

An easy and ancient way of making beads is to use just paper and paste. Cut a strip of paper into a long, thin triangle. Wind this triangular strip around a knitting needle (diagram 37). When a single wind has been completed soak the inside of the rest of the strip in wallpaper paste and continue winding. When the knitting needle has been removed you will have a long thin bead; rounder beads will require a longer strip. The beads can be painted and varnished when dry.

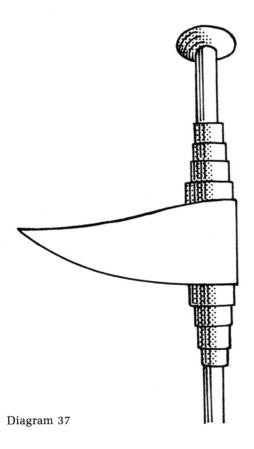

Diagram 37

The Uses of Hand-made Beads

Ceramic beads are strong, water resistant and heavy. They are suitable for all outdoor hangings and articles that require washing. They can support heavy weights and will hold a hanging cord straight if knotted on the end of it.

Beads constructed of cold clay should not be required to bear any heavy weights. A coating of waterproof varnish on the surface of the bead will allow it to be wiped clean. It should not be immersed in water because even if it has been varnished it would be difficult to ascertain that the interior of the bead had also been completely waterproofed. Beads made of cold clay can be used in sculptural forms, jewellery and indoor hangings.

Papier mâché beads are strong and lightweight; they should be treated in the same way as beads made of cold clay. Papier mâché beads are excellent for using in bead curtains, wall hangings and jewellery.

Attaching Beads to Macramé

Beads are generally added to the body of a piece of macramé by threading them on the working or filler cords. Here they can be held in place by a knot below (diagram 38) or by a knot both above and below. If a separate leader or other cord is added to the piece a bead could be threaded on the end of it, tight against the work, held in place by an overhand knot, and the remaining cord clipped away (diagram 39).

If the hole in the bead is too small for the cord it can safely be enlarged if the bead is made of wood or any other easily worked material. If it is impossible to enlarge the hole the cord may be eased through it if the end of the thread is first dipped into melted wax and shaped into a hard point.

The upper part of 'Moonpool', a hanging table that combines cotton cord with large raku beads, some as large as tennis balls

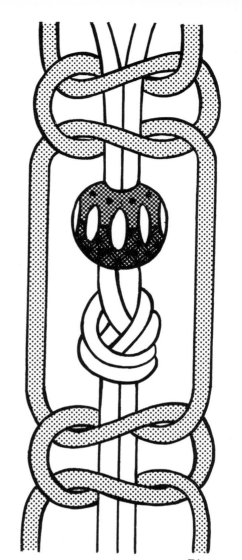

Diagram 38

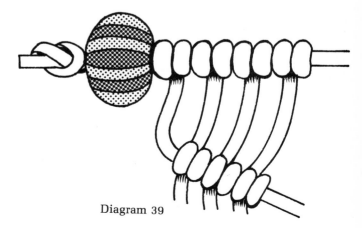

Diagram 39

The tiny bead curtain in the papier mâché
temple was knotted in waxed thread and
decorated with mother-of-pearl, wood and glass
beads. The pinnacles on the columns are carved
bone beads wired together

9 Jewellery

Incorporating Different Media into the Macramé Jewellery

Small is considered beautiful and small items of macramé are no exception to this rule, for some of the most delicate and intricate knotting can be seen worked into tiny pieces of jewellery. Jewellery, naturally, needs to be worked in very fine materials. Waxed nylon threads, macramé twine and lurex threads are all suitable for this type of knotting.

Usually the macramé surface acts as a support for beads and other decorations that are threaded into it. Beads and decorations can create the mood of a piece of jewellery. To explain this I have knotted three macramé necklaces, each with the same formal pattern but changing the ornaments on each one. The photographs of the necklaces, each with a bib-shaped basic design, show how each one has a distinctive character and, as you can see from these examples, it is possible to use a wide variety of decorative elements as part of your jewellery. These can be very natural and simple objects like shells, seeds and small pebbles, or sophisticated ones using semi-precious stones, silver shapes and cloisonné beads. (Cloisonné is the technique of enclosing and dividing coloured enamels from one another with strips of metal.)

Two necklaces knotted in black macramé twine. 'The Travellers' has silver shapes, made by Michael Bolton, knotted into the design and 'Web' is decorated with a cloisonné bead

There is also another way of using macramé in jewellery that will highlight the decorative quality of the knots without using beads. The body of the article (e.g. the circlet of a bracelet) is made in papier mâché and the knotted cord is glued to the surface of the piece and forms its decorative element, making a firm and solid piece of jewellery. The following project is made in this way.

Project: Turk's Head Torc Necklace and Bracelet

Made in Papier Mâché and Macramé

The necklace is based upon a design that goes back at least 3000 years. In pagan times the Gods were portrayed wearing sacred torc necklaces. This project describes the making of a torc and its matching bracelet using macramé and papier mâché.

MATERIALS

60cm (2ft) thick wire. (Coathanger wire is suitable.)

13.5m (14yd 27in) 5–ply 5mm ($\frac{1}{5}$in) thick cord

A piece of thin card approx. 30 × 4cm (12 ×1½in)

Small quantity of torn newspaper strips

Small quantity of papier mâché pulp made with glue

Undercoat paint

Gold picture frame paint (liquid leaf)

Glue

Wallpaper paste

METHOD

Necklace

1 Cut two lengths of cord each 5m (5yd 17in) long and two lengths of cord each 1m (39in) long.

2 Bend 2.5cm (1in) of the ends of the piece of wire back on themselves. Coat the wire with varnish to prevent rusting.

3 Fasten both the 5m (5yd 17in) cords at their centres to one end of the wire (4 working cords). Tie a Chinese crown

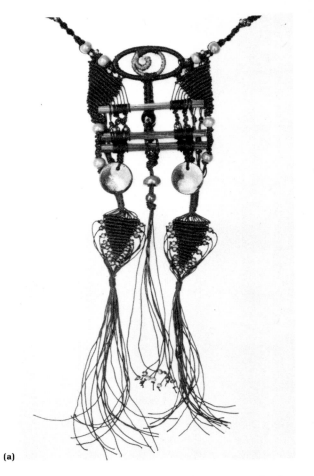

(a)

sinnet the full length of the wire with the wire passing through the centre of the sinnet. Fasten the cord to the far end of the wire, snipping off any excess cord.

4 Mould a ball of papier mâché pulp to each end of the wire with the ends of the sinnet inside it. Leave until the pulp is hard.

5 Bend the wire into the shape of a torc – see photograph of necklace – to fit around the neck. Make sure that the opening is large enough to enable the necklace to be put on and removed without bending it, because the torc will be completely stiff when it is finished.

6 Soak the Chinese crown sinnet in a mixture of glue and wallpaper paste and leave until it is firmly set.

7 Tie a single turk's head knot at the end of a 1m (39in) length of cord. Glue this knot

68

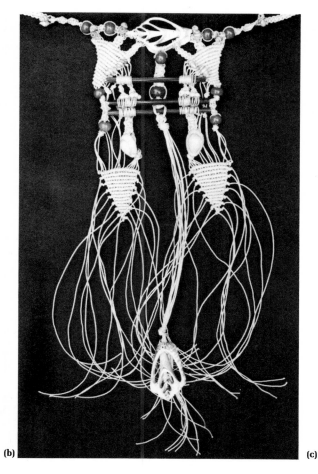

(b)

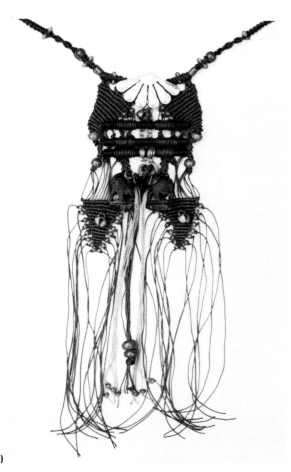

(c)

onto the top of the papier mâché knob at one end of the torc. Snip off the short end of the cord and glue it out of sight behind the back of the knob. With the other end of the cord glue and wrap it round the knob until the join of the papier mâché and the Chinese crown sinnet is covered (see diagram 40). Trim off the excess cord, tuck in the end and glue it in place under the wrap. Repeat with other 1m (39in) cord at the other end.

8 Paint the turk's head knot and wrap with a solution of glue and wallpaper paste and leave to dry.

9 Paint the necklace with a coat of sealing paint followed by a coat of gold paint.

Three necklaces knotted in the same design with different decorations:

(a) 'The eye of Horus' has a wrapped Egyptian charm as a central ornament and its pendant decorations are two enamel plaques. The hanging cords below the pendants have been wrapped above and below the triangular area to give a more formal arrangement to the piece

(b) 'Sea Sampion' is a lighter, more delicate version of the necklace. Extra square knots have been added at the top to compensate for the shallowness of the central ornament. Many of the beads and all of the ornaments are shells or slices of shell

(c) The orient was the inspiration for this exotic variation, 'Calcutta'. The long beads are bamboo; as they are shorter than the glass beads on the other two necklaces 'Calcutta' is narrower and more compact. Minute Indian bells are added to the central panel and the two bottom sections. The hanging pendants are carved wooden elephants whose trunks support some of the central hanging threads

Bracelet

1 Join the ends of the piece of card together adjusting the size to fit an arm.

2 Cover the card with pasted strips of newspaper building up the centre of the outside of the card with a few extra layers of newsprint.

3 Leave to dry over a glass jar or other circular object.

4 Using a 1.5m (1yd 23in) cord, knot a series of turk's head knots around the outer circumference of the bracelet, winding an extra loop of cord around both top and bottom of the turk's head knot circlet. Glue all knots into position. Trim off excess cord and glue the loose ends of the cords under the knots. Leave until the glue is dry.

5 Paint the bracelet first with a sealing paint and then with gold paint.

Diagram 40   This end of the torc necklace shows how the turk's head knot is attached to the papier mâché knob

Earrings can also be made in macramé. This simple pendant design could be made in either thin leather thonging or stiff metallic thread

The turk's head torc and bracelet made in papier mâché and macramé

A superb heavy silver and opal pendant by
Michael Bolton is suspended from a silk and
leather macramé chain

10 Garments

Suitable Materials

Although macramé does not at first seem as suitable a medium for making clothing as, for example, knitting and crochet, it is possible to make quite a large selection of original clothing by this knotting method. Overdresses, capes, men's and women's sweaters, babies layettes, shawls and even bikinis have all been made entirely in macramé.

The most suitable materials for knotted garments are wool, cotton, silk and leather. Jute can be used but owing to its abrasive qualities it is suitable only for garments that do not touch the skin. Leather thonging can be knotted into the most fashionable garments but as it is bulky it is better to knot only part of a leather garment. A glacé leather cape, for example, could have the bottom third of it knotted and fringed in matching or contrasting suede thongs and its front decorated with open turk's head knots. A waistcoat could be embellished with macramé rawhide thonging panels down its front.

Wool is the material to use for soft jumpers and babies' garments, both of which would look attractive worked in sampler fashion showing a variety of different knots. Cotton could be used in the same way for a less expensive garment while an article of clothing made in silk would look most luxurious. Mixtures of wool, silk, cotton, etc. can produce an unusual tactile surface to a garment.

If the sinnets on 'Beachcomber' were lengthened it could be used as an overdress

Above:
'Beachcomber' is an overtunic constructed of square knot sinnets worked with silk, linen, jute and cotton cords. It is decorated with shells and pebbles

Right:
A jute overtunic, tied at the sides with jute cords, is knotted in rust, purple and white with striped bead decoration

Clothing made in macramé should be very simply designed and constructed; plackets and pleats would look far too bulky in a knotted fabric. The natural way of fastening a macramé garment is by incorporating ties into the piece. These could be in the form of a sinnet, a leather thong or simply a single cord, all of which could be decorated Indian fashion with beads, tassels, holed coins or other small ornaments. Another fastening could be made by making buttons out of monkey's fist knots or button knots on one side of an opening and knotting a series of loops on the other.

Garments are usually made on the working board. A simple pattern is selected and drawn in outline on the board. The garment is then knotted within the confines of the guide lines. In order to make working as easy as possible the board need only be large enough to accommodate the front piece of the garment. When the front is finished the drawing of the front is substituted for one of the back which can then also be worked. If the back and the front are to be knotted together across the shoulders, the front (when finished) should be rolled up, put in a plastic bag to keep it clean, and pinned to the top of the board. The back, joined by the shoulders, can then be worked downwards from it.

Garments can be knotted on the board in a variety of different stitches. Tight square knots will give a rich, tapestry-like surface, clove hitches will make the garment firmer and can form elaborate, linear patterns and a three-dimensional effect can be achieved with square knot buttons.

Knotted garments combine quite happily with all types of beads, pearls, charms, very small pebbles, shells, sequins and other haberdashery ornaments, but be subtle in your use of them. Choose, where possible, lightweight decorations as garments can easily be pulled out of shape if heavy baubles are suspended on them.

The back of 'Chinese Harlequin'

Project: Chinese Harlequin Waistcoat

Made in Leather

A sleeveless waistcoat of loose, suede diamond shapes, coloured in ochre, ivory, beige, rust, green and brown, laced together with leather thongs in a pattern of chinese crown knots, overhand knots and tassels. All sizes. Length 48cm (19in)

MATERIALS

1 piece of thin suede large enough for the back, divided in half down the centre

28 diamonds of thin suede 12 × 25cm (4¾ × 10in) + 1cm (⅜in) turn in all the way round. (All suede should be thin enough not to need paring. Diamonds to be assorted colours)

84 pieces of thonging 40cm (16in) long. To use less thonging see stage 4

METHOD

1 Make a full size pattern from diagrams 41 and 42 adjusting to fit sizes other than size 12. Length to remain the same as in the pattern.

2 Mitre the turnings on the diamonds, turn down the 1cm (⅜in) turnings to the underside and secure either by sewing or using a flexible adhesive, make sure that it is one that would allow the garment to be dry cleaned. Punch a hole in every corner of 27 diamonds.

3 Position 26 diamonds – do not include the one without holes – in two rectangles of 2½ diamonds wide × 2½ diamonds long, cutting the diamonds in halves and quarters where necessary (see diagram 43). Fasten these diamonds to each other in the following way:
a Place two wet leather thongs right side down onto a working board crossed at their centres and secured with a pin.
b Tie a chinese crown knot around the pin. Remove the thong and leave to dry.

Right:
The suede diamonds on this garment are knotted together with leather thongs in a pattern of Chinese crown and overhand knots

Diagram 41 (top, this page) **Front waistcoat pattern. Enlarge two small squares to 2.5cm (1in) to make a size 12 pattern. Adjust for larger sizes**

Diagram 42 (top, following page) **Back waistcoat pattern**

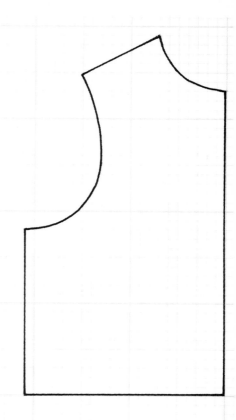

c Thread the thongs through three of the four holes in the corners of the touching diamonds from front to back, leaving the bottom thong and hole. Centre the chinese crown knot in the middle of the four holes.

d Thread all three thongs from back to front through the bottom hole. Tie an overhand knot with all four thongs. When there are less than four holes use the vacant space as if it were a hole.

e Trim ends to make a tassel 5cm (2in) long.

4 When all the diamonds have been joined together cut the two fronts out of the rectangles. In order to use less thonging first fasten the diamonds together with twine and then cut out the shape. Replace only the knots that are on the cut-out fronts with leather thongs.

5 Cut out the back from the large piece of suede and divide down the centre back. Turn in centre back edges and secure.

6 Place the two back pieces together and position the remaining two diamonds one above the other over the centre back. The diamond with no holes in it should be at the bottom and can now have the top three holes punched in it (see diagram 44). Mark and pierce holes in the back pieces to correspond with the pattern of holes on the front (also diagram 44).

7 Tie the two diamonds to the back pieces with Chinese crown and overhand knots as with the front.

8 Sew the waistcoat together at the shoulder and sides and sew together any loose pieces of diamond at the armhole edges and neckline (marked *X* on diagram 43). Turn in and secure all raw edges.

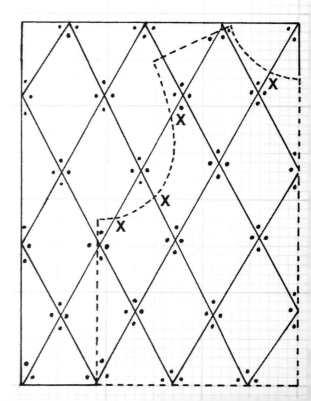

Diagram 43

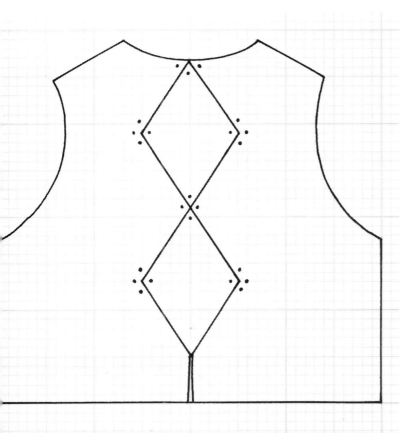

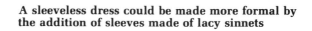

A sleeveless dress could be made more formal by the addition of sleeves made of lacy sinnets

A detail of the knot and tassel

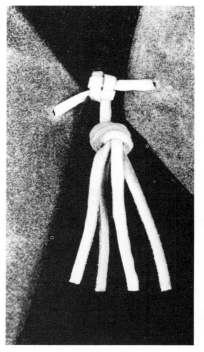

Diagram 44

11 Accessories

Day and Evening Wear and Animal Accessories

The versatility of macramé is nowhere better illustrated than in making accessories. The use to which the accessory is put is largely governed by the materials with which it is made. Thus a bag and belt made of leather thongs would be suitable for outdoor, everyday use and a set worked in gold or silver cord with a beaded trim would make an excellent evening accessory.

The most popular macramé accessory in use today is the string shopping bag. It is easy to pack away when not needed and when it is full it is very strong and hardwearing. A shopping bag in string could be simply worked in an alternate square knot pattern or be quite boldly patterned with a decoration of berry knots and clove hitches. Smaller articles like handbags and belts can be made to match each other by giving emphasis to the same series of knots in each accessory and also by matching the belt buckle to the handbag handles. Buckles and handles can be bought in many haberdashery shops but are not always necessary, for a belt can be made long enough to be used as a sash tied round the waist and bags can be slung from worked macramé handles. Bag and belt accessories need not just be for women; a leather thonged belt would be a useful addition to any man's wardrobe. Many men find a pouch bag useful in summer when they don't wear a jacket, and this made in leather thonging would be a simple macramé article to make.

Macramé accessories for day wear, as well as the aforementioned belts and bags, include sandal and boot tops, hats and caps, both men's and women's braces (either decorative or useful), headbands, ties and watchstraps. For evenings elaborate and colourful beads can be added to cords made of silk, metallic thread or gold or silver gimp to make belts, bags, headgear and sandal-tops that will enliven even the plainest of evening dresses.

There are also other kinds of accessories that up to now have been rather neglected and these are the ones used in connection with your pets. Why not make a cat collar, a dog lead or one of the many articles that would be useful when attending to your horse or pony? A dog lead would be very strong and inexpensive if made in jute or string. A leather lead would look more attractive, but

Left:
A sash, cap and handbag knotted in a soft, grey-green wool. All are decorated with hand-made ceramic beads and the handbag has a large, matching ceramic button

Right:
A leather thong dog lead knotted in Chinese crown knots and square knots

thonging is not very strong so the lead would need an inner core of strong cord like one made of woven nylon.

There are many uses in stables for macramé, for example hay nets, girths, reins, all-purpose leading and tying ropes and perhaps the most useful, from the horse's point of view, the fly fringe.

Project I: Sioux Belt and Pouch

Made in Wool (or Jute) and Leather
The pouch is decorated in leather thonging and carried on the belt, and is a useful accessory for carrying a wallet or any other small item. It can be made in two versions: one, made in heavy, non-elastic wool, leather thongs and beads can be used by a woman, while the other, plainer version, made in 3-ply jute and leather, is suitable for a man.

Belt

MATERIALS

2 curtain rings approx. 5cm (2in) in diameter

2.5m (2yd 26in) of thonging

6 cords in wool or jute (both hereafter described as cord) each with a length of eight times the waist measurement plus 2m (2yd 7in) each cord

METHOD

1 Wrap the two curtain rings with leather thonging; glue thonging in position.

2 Attach the six cords by lark's head knots at their centres around both the rings, fastening them together (12 working cords).

3 Work a sinnet of alternate square knots by repeating the following two rows:
1st row – three square knots
2nd row – two floating cords, two square knots, two floating cords

---

The girl in this sketch holds a macramé shoulder bag with a wooden handle. Her sandals have knotted tops

This is the woman's
'Sioux' pouch. It is
knotted in soft wool
with silver leather
thonging and
multi-colour beads

Continue until the work measures the
width of the waist plus 25cm (10in). End
on a row of three square knots.

4 Tie each filler and working cord together
with two overhand knots. Trim ends to
8cm (3¼in) and finish with an overhand
knot.

Pouch

Size: 12 × 12cm (4¾ × 4¾in) without fringe

MATERIALS

Piece of stiff belting 48cm (19in) long

Piece of thin leather 50 × 8cm
(20 × 3¼in) long

1 curtain ring 3cm (1⅛in) in diameter

8 lengths of leather thonging 1.3m
(1yd 15in) long

4 lengths of leather thonging 12cm
(4¾in) long

175m (190yd) cord

10 globular and pendant beads (for the
woman's pouch)

METHOD

1 Cut the following lengths of cord:

54 cords each 3m (3yd 10in) long
1 cord 11m (12yd) long (gusset)
1 cord 1m (1yd 3in) long (button)
2 cords 30cm (1ft) long (leader cords)

2 Wrap and glue the 50cm (20in) piece of leather, edges to the centre on the inside, around the belting. This is the gusset of the pouch (see diagram 45 for stages 2–7).

3 Pierce four holes at each end in the leather strip 7cm (2¾in) from the end and equidistant from each other. The two 7cm (2¾in) ends form the inner flaps of the purse. Trim the leather edges of the flaps so that they just cover the belting.

4 Glue two 12cm (4¾in) lengths of thonging together to form one of the two loops that thread the pouch onto the belt. Thread the ends of the loop through the inner holes at one end of the gusset; glue firmly, with a strong adhesive, the ends of the loops to the inside of the gusset. Open its glued inner central join in order to do this and glue the join back in position again. Repeat at the other end.

5 Thread the 11m (12yd) cord through the two holes that are used for the loop at one end of the gusset and adjust the cord until both ends are the same length. Using the gusset as a filler cord and the two 5.5m (6yd) cords as working cords, work a square knot sinnet until it reaches the loop at the other end. Here the ends of the cord are passed through the loop holes, fastened off and trimmed.

6 Using one cord 30cm (1ft) long pass it through the front outer hole at both ends of the gusset and tie its ends together to form a double foundation cord 12cm (4¾in) long. Trim off the end and repeat with the other 30cm (1ft) cord and the two back holes.

7 On the front foundation cord attach by lark's head knots at their centres 18 cords 3m (3yd 10in) long (36 working cords) and work a panel of alternate square knots for 12cm (4¾in). While working this panel slip the outermost cord at each end through one of the square knot loops on the gusset each time you knot a row, thus fastening the front and the sides together.

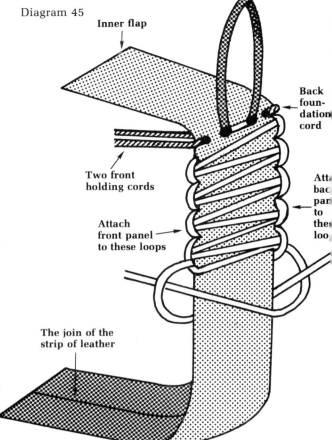

Diagram 45

Inner flap

Back foundation cord

Two front holding cords

Attach front panel to these loops

Atta bac pan to thes loo

The join of the strip of leather

8 Thread the 36 cords through the front of the square knot loops on the part of the gusset that forms the base of the bag. Tie another row of square knots and fasten off as in stage 3 of the belt. Make a 12cm (4¾in) long fringe.

9 On the back foundation cord attach at each end eight cords 3m (3yd 10in) long by clove hitches at their centres. (This makes one cord go upwards to form the flap and the other cord go downwards to form the back of the pouch.) Inside these cords, at each end attach a 1.3m (1yd 15in) leather thong by a lark's head knot at its centre to the back foundation cord;

position it upwards to become part of the flap. Attach one 3m (3yd 10in) long cord (with a lark's head knot at its centre positioned downwards to form part of the back) at each end next to the leather thong. Alternating leather and cord, repeat until four leather thongs and three single cords are attached to the foundation cord at each end. Attach eight cords 3m (3yd 10in) long by clove hitches to the foundation cord in the centre of the pouch. When all cords and thongs are attached there should be 36 cords positioned downwards, and 24 cords and 16 thongs positioned upwards to form the flap. Diagram 46 shows quite clearly how these cords are attached.

10 Work the back of the pouch the same as the front but make the fringe 14cm (5½in) long.

11 Work the flap in alternate square knots for 8cm (3¼in).

12 On the eight cords at each end work an alternate square knot sinnet for 7cm (2¾in) ending as for the belt but with a 15cm (6in) fringe.

13 On the central set of eight cords also work a 7cm (2¾in) alternate square knot sinnet ending with two square knots. Work a five-knot square knot sinnet with each set of four cords to form the button hole. On the eight cords leave two floating cords, work one square knot and finish with two floating cords. Finish as for the belt but with a fringe of 15cm (6in).

14 On one set of eight leather thongs – using the outer thong as a leader cord – work a row of clove hitches. Using the two central thongs as leaders work a diamond pattern of clove hitches using all the thongs.

15 On the woman's pouch thread a bead on the two central thongs and one on each group of three thongs. Finish both men's and women's pouches with overhand knots on the end of the cords. Trim the outer thongs to a length of 5cm (2in) and the two central thongs in each leather strip to a length of 7cm (2¾in). Tie a pendant bead onto each of these two cords on the woman's pouch.

Button

Make a button similar to a Dorset cross-wheel button by wrapping the small curtain ring with the 1m (39in) length of cord. Make 12 divisions across the circle with this cord and weave the cord in and out of the 12 divisions until the circle is completely filled. Sew the button in position on the pouch which is now ready to be looped over the belt.

Diagram 46 **Half of the cords attached to the foundation cord**

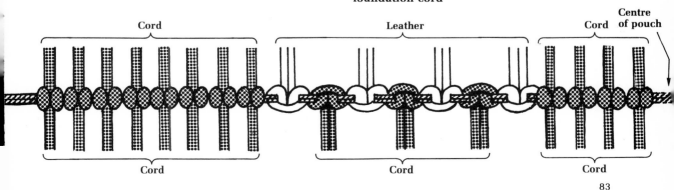

Cord   Leather   Centre
Cord   of pouch

Cord   Cord   Cord

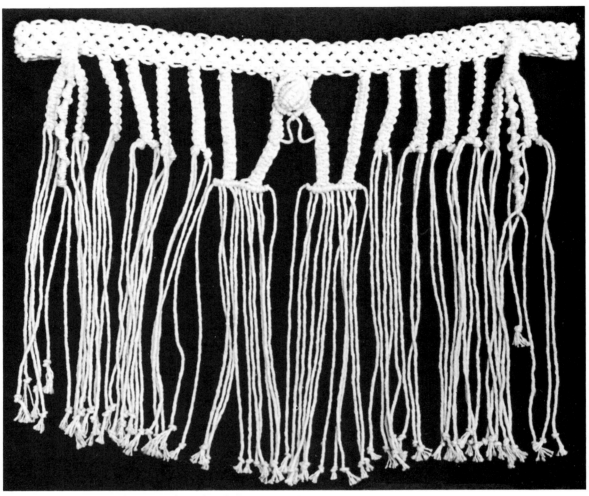

The fly fringe ready to be slid into position on the head-collar

Diagram 47

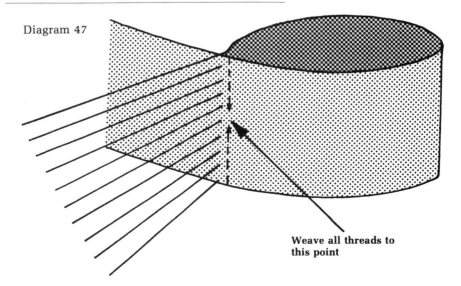

Weave all threads to this point

Project II: Horse's Fly Fringe

Made in Cotton Twine

This fringe used as a brow band on a horse's head-collar when it is turned out to grass in the summer keeps the flies away from the animal's eyes and saves it from a lot of unnecessary suffering. The pattern of the fly fringe shown here is loosely based upon the decorative harness worn by carthorses. If it is knotted in soft cotton twine this fringe will prove to be hard-wearing as well as comfortable for the horse. The pattern is for a full-sized horse (pony size is in brackets) taking the width across the brow for a horse as 40cm (16in) and for a pony as 32cm (12½in).

MATERIALS

69.5m (76yd 19in) cotton twine

METHOD

1 Cut the following lengths of cord:
   1 cord 4m (4yd 13in) long
   9 cords 3m (3yd 10in) long
   5 cords 2.5m (2yd 26in) long
   10 cords 1.5m (1yd 23in) long
   10 cords 1m (1yd 3in) long
   2 cords 50cm (20in) long

2 Working with nine cords 3m (3yd 10in) long and one cord 4m (4yd 13in) long, leave 60cm (2ft) of cord free at one end of all the 3m (3yd 10in) cords and 1.1m (1yd 7in) free on the 4m (4yd 13in) cord at the same end. Work alternate square knots with these ten cords for 46cm (18in) (38cm (15in)). Turn 3cm (1½in) of each end back upon itself to the back of the strip and, using a large darning needle, thread all the cords from the back through the knotting to the front. Weave the top threads downwards and the bottom ones up until all threads come from the centre (see diagram 4). At each end make a 3.5cm (1½in) square knot sinnet with two working cords; use the rest, including the 4m (4yd 13in) cord, as fillers.

The horse is wearing the fly fringe and is held by a macramé leading rope

3 At each end of the brow band pull the 4m (4yd 13in) cord to the centre of the sinnet and use it as a working cord to knot a twisting half hitch sinnet 10cm (4in) long around another central cord. Finish by tying each filling and working cord together with two overhand knots. On each side of this half hitch sinnet work a 5cm (2in) square knot sinnet using two working and two filling cords, finishing as above.

4 At the centre of the band attach, by lark's head knots at their centres to the loops formed by the alternate square knot pattern, five cords 2.5m (2yd 26in) long (ten working cords). With these ten cords tie a berry knot surrounded by a circle of clove hitches. Work half the clove hitch circle, then the berry knot followed by the other half circle. Leave the two centre cords and with the four cords on either side knot two square knot sinnets 3cm (1¼in) long. Add one of the central cords to each sinnet and continue sinnets for another 3.5cm (1½in).

5 Approx. 2.5cm (1in) from the berry knot add on each side one cord 1.5m (1yd 23in) long and one cord 1m (1yd 3in)

long by lark's head knots at their centres to the loops on the bottom of the brow band. Using the longer cords as the working cords (always do this unless otherwise stated) make a 9cm (3½in) square knot sinnet. On each side of the brow band join this sinnet to the square knot sinnet beside it by using each 50cm (20in) cord as a holding cord for a row of clove hitches across all nine cords. Secure the holding cord by an overhand knot at each end.

6 In each remaining space on either side add (by lark's head knots at their centres) to the bottom loops four groups, evenly spaced, of one cord 1m (1yd 3in) long and one cord 1.5m (1yd 23in) long. With each group make a 5cm (2in) square knot sinnet finishing as in stage 3.

7 Trim all cords to a length of 28cm (11in) finishing each with an overhand knot. The fly fringe is threaded onto the head collar through the 3cm (1¼in) loops at either end.

A man's belt in heavy leather is decorated with a thonging overlay of square knots

12 Plant Hangings, Wind-chimes and Bells

Anyone today can buy a macramé plant hanging as they are easily obtainable in most florists and craft shops. However, it can be much more original and more satisfying to make an individual plant hanging which, in both colour and design, would suit the specific requirements of your home.

A plant hanging is basically a simple macramé construction of four or more sinnets pendant from a ring or chain. The sinnets are knotted at the bottom to form a cradle (diagram 48) which supports the plant pot. Sometimes, instead of forming a cradle, the sinnets are clove-hitched onto a ring which acts as a support for the base of the pot. This is the best design to use if the pot has a pronounced foot-ring (the ridge at the bottom of a pot that enables it to stand upright).

Combining Plants, Pots and Macramé

One of the primary considerations when designing a plant hanging is that the plant pot, hanging and plant should together form a single, harmonious unit. Take as much care in choosing the plant container as you would in making the hanging. If you have a plant pot that is well worth displaying, make sure that the hanging blends with it in both style and colour. For example, a typically-shaped Chinese pot in white or celadon grey would show to advantage with a lacquer red oriental style of hanging, while a roughly-shaped primitive pot would look best with a hanging in a rough, natural material like jute or handspun fleece. Jute and other natural fibres combine well with

both oxidized and reduced stoneware and terracotta pottery; a shiny blue rayon thread would suit the popular blue and white ceramics while copper, brass and any other metal containers deserve heavier hangings, possibly in leather or waxed cord.

Care should be taken in the colour of the hanging. Remember that the hanging and the pot are there to support the plant and show off the beauty of its flowers and leaves. Plants that are kept for the decorative shape of their green leaves would look

Diagram 48   **A typical cradle for holding a plant pot**

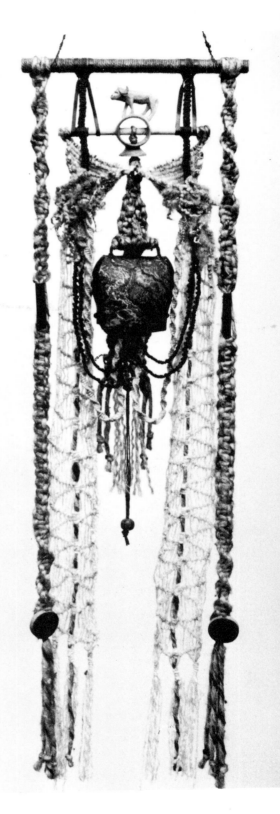

attractive with any brightly-coloured hanging and pot, but gay plants with brightly-coloured flowers, especially the magenta ones, would certainly look their best in a plain container supported by a hanging in green or natural cord.

Bells

Decorative hangings can also support wind-chimes or bells which, hung outdoors or near an open window, would not only look interesting but make a soft, musical sound as well. Bells in china, metal and glass can be incorporated into macramé. In fact one of the earliest uses of macramé on board ship was when it was made into a heavy bell pull attached to the clapper of the ships bell. An attractive way of hanging a bell would be to suspend it from a decorative strip of macramé with a smaller matching bell pull hung from its clapper. Bells are also easily incorporated into much larger pieces of macramé, such as wall hangings, where they can give a nautical feeling to the piece.

Wind-Chimes

While bells generally have to be bought, wind-chimes are very much less expensive as they can be made from many different oddments. Most objects that make a pleasing sound when gently blown together by the wind can be made into a chime. Large mother-of-pearl discs, smooth edged pieces of glass, bamboo and glass beads and tubular pieces of steel are all suitable, providing there is a way of attaching them to a cord. Here too is a use for a pot that has collapsed whilst being thrown. Leave it until it is leather hard, cut up the thinnest parts into random shapes, make a hole in each and smooth down the sharp edges; biscuit fire them, glaze and fire, and you have the makings of a wind-chime.

Left:
A group of plant hangings

'Buffalo Bell', a hanging in linen, chenille and cotton cords decorated with a large cow bell, pieces of fleece and a carved serviette ring

The two projects described here are both simple to make. The hangings require a relatively small amount of cord, and craft potters should find no difficulty in making the pot, saucer and beads. For those without access to a kiln the floral beads and pottery could also be made in papier mâché that has been given a waterproof finish. Suitably shaped pots and saucers are obtainable in most china shops. Japanese shops, in particular, stock some very decorative shallow, lotus-shaped bowls. The saucer should alway be watertight but if the pot used in the design 'Geisha' is porous remember to make the hanging of rot-proof cord.

A pot based upon the design of a Greek amphora carried here would look striking if the pot were supported about half-way up by a ring suspended on a macramé hanging

Project I: Geisha Plant Pot Hanging
Made in Cord with a Variety of Pots

An all-purpose plant hanging. The plant can be planted directly into the pot or put in a small, concealed container. This design can also double as a vase for flowers or dried grasses. The hanging, which is knotted in thick, white cord, features lovers' knots and the pot it supports is made in lustre raku. The macramé, unlike most hangings, is worked from the bottom upwards.

MATERIALS

29.5m (32yd 10in) cord, medium to thick 3–5mm (⅛–¼in)

1 plant pot approx. 20cm (8in) in diameter

2 brass curtain rings 3.5cm (1½in) in diameter

METHOD

1 Cut eight cords 3.5m (3yd 30in) long and one cord 1.5m (1yd 23in) long.

2 Attach the eight cords by lark's head knots at their centres to one of the brass rings (16 working cords).

3 Using two working and two filler cords make a square knot with each set of four cords. Leave 5cm (2in) of cord unknotted.

4 Taking two cords from one square knot and two from the one next to it tie two square knots. Repeat with the rest of the cords. Leave 10cm (4in) of cord unknotted.

5 Taking two cords from one square knot and two from the one next to it tie a lover's knot with double cords. Repeat with the rest of the cords; four lovers' knots in all.

Left:
A group of bells showing just a few of the many types of bell available nowadays

Far left:
'Geisha', shown here in the middle of the photograph supporting a raku coil pot, can also be used with a papier mâché balloon pot. A slight adjustment in the length of the cords between the knots makes this design suitable to hold a wooden kitchen sieve (seen on the left of the photograph), which makes an unusual plant holder

6 Leave 70cm (28in) of cord unknotted. Using eight cords as working cords and eight cords as fillers, tie one square knot. Thread the filler cords through the second brass ring and tie another square knot.

7 Fold the second square knot over against the first so that the brass ring is at the top to form the loop for hanging.

8 Spread all the cord ends evenly around the 70cm (28in) unknotted hanging cords and fasten them all together with a 6cm (2¼in) wrap knot using the 1.5m (1yd 23in) cord for this purpose. Trim the loose ends to a length of 12cm (4¾in) and separate the plies of the cords to make a tassel.

Project II: Daisy Chain Saucer Hanging
Made in Ceramic or Papier Mâché and Wool

A delicate hanging that supports a saucer for a plant pot. This project is knotted in a soft, green non-stretch wool and decorated with porcelain beads made in the shape of daisies. The pale green saucer is also made of porcelain and embellished with the daisy motif.

MATERIALS

1 deep saucer approx. 20cm (8in) in diameter

1 wooden ring 5.5cm (2¼ins) in diameter

7 daisies or other floral beads

68m (74yd 9in) of 5mm (¼in) wool

METHOD

1 Cut eight cords 8m (8yd 25in) long and four cords 1m (1yd 3in) long.

2 Put the eight long cords together and locate their centre point. Starting 5cm (2in) from the centre make a 10cm (4in)

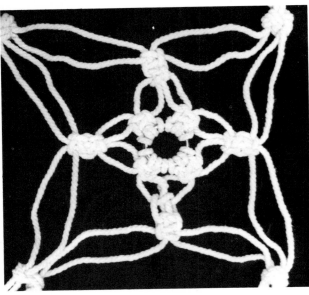

Top left:
The top of 'Geisha'

Left:
The bottom of 'Geisha'

Right:
'Daisy Chain'

long square knot sinnet using two of the 1m (1yd 3in) cords as working cords and the eight long cords as fillers. The sinnet should be in the exact centre of the long cords.

3 Fold the sinnet in half over the ring and fasten it in position by tying a 5cm (2in) long wrap around all the cords using a 1m (1yd 3in) cord. Clip off the ends of the 1m (1yd 3in) cords below the wrap leaving 16 working cords.

4 Divide the cords into four groups of four cords and tie a 10cm (4in) long Chinese crown sinnet, using each group of four cords as if it were one cord.

5 Separate the cords, and using four single cords tie a 20cm (8in) long bannister bar. Thread on a floral bead, reverse working and filler cords and tie a 16cm (6¼in) long square knot sinnet.

6 Repeat stage 5 with the other three groups of cords making four holding straps.

7 On all straps leave 10cm (4in) of cord unknotted. Take two cords from one group and two from the group next to it and tie two square knots with these four cords. Repeat until all cords have been knotted.

8 Leave 5cm (2in) of cord unknotted and with the last 1m (1yd 3in) cord tie a 5cm (2in) wrap knot around all the cords. Trim the tassel to a length of 25cm (10in) and decorate with the three remaining floral beads, fastening each into position with an overhand knot. With a small piece of wool thread the four beads on the sinnets together and fasten off neatly and invisibly.

The daisies

The daisies were made in a sprig mould. This is a small block of plaster with a design, modelled in shallow relief, impressed into it. The daisy is made by pressing papier mâché or clay (see press moulding in Chapter 8) into the daisy-shaped depression in the plaster, smoothing the back flat and immediately removing. If two daisy casts are bent into a slight curve and joined together at their edges a cord can be threaded through them. Sprig moulds can be obtained from leading manufacturers of craft pottery equipment.

Above:
A close up of the chime showing the glass beads and button knots

Right:
'Wind Chime', a plant holder using a similar design to 'Daisy Chain'

Project III: Wind-Chime

Work the macramé hanging as for the 'Daisy Chain' except that the square knot sinnet and the bannister bar are reversed and the central beads are not caught together. This hanging is knotted in green jute with bottle green glass beads instead of daisies separating the sinnets. The tassel is further decorated with large square knot buttons, long glass beads and three sizes of globular bead in blue and green glass. The saucer has a blue and green geometric pattern on its inside.

13 Hanging Tables and Dishes

Design of Hanging Tables

A hanging table is an extremely versatile article which can be equally at home in a porch, patio or garden. Hung from a tree it will make a bird table that very few cats can reach or, used indoors as a small occasional table, it will enliven a dull corner of any room. It would be an especially useful item if the floor is stepped or uneven. Hanging tables and dishes which combine both macramé and ceramics show how easily the two crafts can support and enhance each other. The examples depicted here have been designed to integrate both simple and elaborate mixtures of hanging and ceramics. Each must be considered carefully in relation to the other if a balanced result is to be achieved. Generally, a satisfactory effect will be obtained if either the ceramic or the hanging is simply constructed, setting off the more elaborate decoration on the other. However, both could be decorative if one echoed the design of the other; for example, a complex macramé pattern based on square knots could be partnered by a tabletop with a brushed oxide design of a large square knot painted on its upper surface. Another way of integrating pottery and macramé is for the hanging to exactly match the colour of one of the glazes used on the surface of the table. It is often better to use only one colour of macramé for each hanging as the overall outline tends to get lost if the knotting is striped; small areas, though, like the wraps on tassels, can look most attractive in a contrasting colour.

This rustic table combines a roughly shaped piece of wood with jute cords and wooden beads

Above:
Two decorative tabletop designs. The top is based on a classical Greek design and would be suitable to be painted onto the surface of a papier mâché tabletop. The other is from a seventeenth-century English slipware dish and would be suitable as decoration on an earthenware tabletop

Left:
Two hanging dishes. The hanging on the front dish is knotted in black glossy cord and the dish itself is finished in a combination of unglazed terracotta and black lustre glaze. The small dish at the back is glazed in brown, black and white. Its hanging is stiff, brown rot-proof cord

Wood and Papier Mâché Tabletops

Ceramic dishes and tabletops can be any curved shape–round, oval, kidney or free form – but ceramic materials are not entirely suitable for a straight-sided table. It would be better in this case to have a table made of wood which could either be polished or left untreated. Wood is an excellent material to use in the making of hanging tables and dishes as it is easy to bore the holes in it necessary for the hanging's supporting cords. A table made from a slice of untrimmed wood would make an attractive rustic hanging, especially if combined with macramé worked in natural jute, and a shallow turned dish would also harmonize with this type of cord.

A tabletop can also be made of papier mâché, which has the advantage of being lightweight and therefore suitable for a supporting beam that is not very strong. These tabletops can also have a waterproof finish that enables them to be left outdoors.

The table's knotted hanging consists of a ring at the top holding three or more decorative sinnets, which pass through holes pierced or drilled through the tabletop or dish and are knotted on the underside in a variety of different ways. They are usually wrapped together to form a tassel in the centre, which gives the table extra strength. Although three supporting sinnets are probably the best number to hold the table steady – think of a three legged stool – four sinnets can also be used; more tend to obstruct the surface of the table or dish.

As the hanging will often have to support – in the case of ceramics and wood – a fairly heavy weight, it is advisable to use a heavy cord and rings that are made of wood or soldered metal. Plastic rings are not strong enough.

If the table is to be used in the garden, rot-proof cord should be used. It should be mentioned here that any flat ceramic tabletop that does not retain water on its

A simple hanging bird table. The hanging is knotted in cream rot-proof cord and is decorated with ceramic and bamboo beads

E

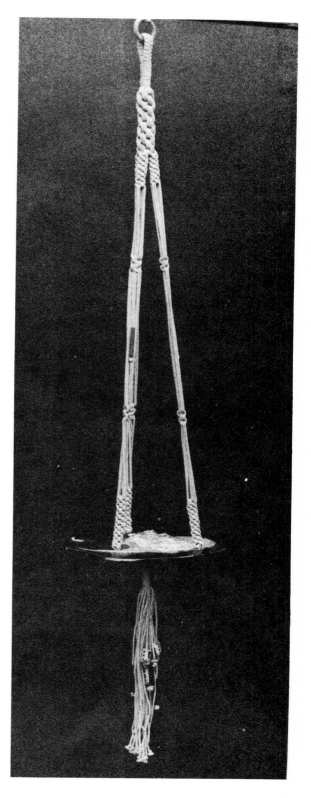

surface can be safely left outside in winter. Any dish or table that does hold water should be brought indoors in very cold weather as the formation of ice in the hollows of the ceramic will cause it to crack.

There are many ways to design, make and decorate a hanging table or dish, and the methods explained here are only a few of the many that can be used. Do not just follow these designs; experiment with any of the different cords, glazes and knots that are available until you are satisfied with the result. Try making a very simple hanging bird table by using the design of 'Daisy Chain' hanging until you reach the instructions for making the cradle. Instead of making this cradle pass the sinnets through the holes in a prepared tabletop and tie in a tassel underneath. Any hanging dish can also be made using these patterns.

Project: Crystal Palace Hanging Table
Made in Ceramic, Wood, or Papier Mâché and Cord

This project has no beads or other decorations. It relies entirely on the sculptural quality of its intricate design carried out in variations of the square knot. The stoneware tabletop, softly glazed in white, pale blue and green, is decorated with a small pierced crescent moon.

MATERIALS

1 kilo (2.2lb) 5mm (⅕in) white cotton twine, 171 metres per kilo (187yd per 2.2lb)

1 ring 15cm (6in) in diameter

1 ring 10cm (4in) in diameter

1 small ring for hanging

1 tabletop in ceramic, wood or papier mâché approx. 35–40cm (14–16in) in diameter pierced with three holes at least 5cm (2in) from the edge of the table

'Crystal Palace' knotted in white twine

METHOD

1 Cut the following lengths of cord:
6 cords 15m (16yd 15in) long
12 cords 1m 50cm (1yd 23in) long
12 cords 5m (5yd 17in) long
2 cords 1m (1yd 3in) long

2 Mount the six cords of 15m (16yd 15in) and the 12 cords of 5m (5yd 17in) on the small ring by folding them in half over the ring and fastening them together with a 5cm (2in) wrap knot using one of the 1m (1yd 3in) cords. Make sure that the long cords are evenly distributed around the wrap knot (36 working cords).

3 Divide the 36 cords into nine groups of four cords, at least one long cord in each group, and make a 10cm (4in) long square knot sinnet with each group.

4 Clove hitch all cords to the 15cm (6in) ring. Divide the cords into three groups of 12 cords each, making sure that there are four of the 15m (16yd 15in) cords in each group. Leave a space between each group of cords on the large ring.

5 Divide one group of 12 cords into three groups of four cords. With each group of four tie a square knot, followed by a sinnet of seven half knots and ending with another square knot. Repeat step 5 with the other two groups of 12 cords.

6 Clove hitch all cords onto the 10 cm (4in) ring. With one group of 12 cords bring the eight short cords to the front, and with each group of four cords make a sinnet of three square knots. Behind these sinnets make a three-square-knot sinnet with the four long cords. Repeat with the other two groups of 12 cords.

7 Leave the 12 long cords and around them form a cylinder by making three rows of alternating square knots with all the shorter cords (24 cords).

8 On the fourth row of the cylinder make a four-knot square knot button with every other square knot (three buttons).

9 Continue alternating square knots for seven more rows.

A detail of the macramé work on 'Crystal Palace'

10 With each group of four cords make a sinnet 10cm (4in) long, alternating the pattern of each sinnet: sinnets 1,3,5 to be square knot sinnets, sinnets 2,4,6 to be bannister bars. Finish by knotting each couple of cords together with two overhand knots. Trim each end to a length of 15cm (6in) with an overhand knot on the end of each.

11 Return to the spaces left on the 15cm (6in) ring in stage 4. Into each space attach by lark's head knots at their centres four cords 1.5m (1yd 23in) long (24 working cords).

12 With each group of eight cords use the four centre cords to make a four-knot square knot button. Divide cords into two groups of four cords and make a four-knot square knot button with each, followed by three square knots. Thread each group of eight cords through the space beneath it below the 10cm (4in) ring. Tuck them out of sight into the centre of the cylinder. From the bottom of the cylinder tie a wrap around these 24 cords out of sight within the cylinder, using the last 1m (1yd 3in) cord. Trim ends of cords close to the wrap. The 12 long cords should be left hanging free and not enclosed in this wrap.

13 With the 12 long cords (the only ones now left) from the bottom of the covering cylinder, make another cylinder by alternating square knots for 15 rows.

14 Divide the 12 cords into three groups of four cords and tie bannister bars for 60cm (2ft).

15 Pass each sinnet through a hole in the table and reverse the filler and working cords. Make a square knot sinnet until the sinnets meet at the centre of the underside of the table.

16 Join the sinnets by making another cylinder of alternate square knots for 10cm (4in). Finish by knotting each couple of knots together using two overhand knots; trim the cords to a length of 20cm (8in). Tie an overhand knot on the end of each.

The bottom of 'Crystal Palace'

14 Macramé as an Art form

Macramé is described as the art of tying knots into a variety of patterns and designs for practical and æsthetic purposes. Up to now in this book the patterns have been designed primarily for their usefulness. However, when macramé is used as an art form its purpose is purely æsthetic. The article created exists for no other purpose than to give pleasure, in the same way as enjoyment can be obtained from viewing a painting of, for example, a landscape. It also adds a richness and texture to its environment because the viewers are also tempted to explore the work using their sense of touch.

Macramé for artistic purposes can be roughly divided into three groups: constructions can be made to be hung on the wall, suspended from the ceiling (mobiles) or be free-standing sculptures.

Wall Hangings

Wall hangings have been used for many centuries. Before our more civilized methods of central heating, hangings were used to help preserve the warmth of a log fire in a room. In royal castles huge woven tapestries were suspended on the walls of state apartments, which not only kept the room warm but were often themselves great works of art. Today hangings are not needed for warmth but it is just as important to have a pleasing environment, and a macramé hanging can help achieve this.

There are two types of hangings: flat hangings, which have little depth and rely

'Agaricus', a sculptural mobile of porcelain shapes strung on bannister bar sinnets

on the pattern of their knots for decoration, and relief hangings, which give a three-dimensional effect by means of raised areas, tubular forms and sinnets that twist and fold over each other. The flat hangings are suitable for door and window hangings; they are usually knotted loosely in order to allow light to penetrate, and are designed for places where a design in deep relief would protrude and get in the way. Wall hangings worked in relief can be any size depending on the wall to be covered; they can be small enought to fit into the most constricted alcove or worked into a large imposing structure that can cover the entire wall. But both flat and relief hangings are extremely interesting to design and make. It is a good idea when starting a hanging to draw a simplified diagram of your design onto a working board at first and to experiment with different kinds of knots, working within the framework of the diagram.

Mobiles

These are either three dimensional or flat pieces of macramé that are hung from the ceiling in such a position that their hanging parts can move and be viewed from all angles. There are a number of different ways in which a mobile can be constructed: it can be worked in a long tubular shape which can act as a framework for interesting beads and other decorations, a number of small hangings can be suspended at various levels from something like a small hoop, or a mobile can be a single construction knotted over a firm foundation like a lampshade frame. Mobiles can also have two or more pieces of macramé suspended one inside the other which can move independently, with inner layers that can be seen through the spaces left in the outer forms. Mobiles, perhaps more than any other art form, allow the artist to explore the relationship between form and space. The spaces between the knotted areas are as important to the design of the piece as the knots themselves, and each must be considered carefully in relation to the other to attain a balanced result.

Above:
'Salome', a macramé and ceramic sculpture. It is a pastiche of the black and white drawings created by Aubrey Beardsley to illustrate Oscar Wilde's *Salome*

Far left:
The girl wearing a dress with a macramé inset and a macramé belt is working on a large wall hanging. It is suspended on two hooks which have been screwed into the top of a doorway

Above:
The start of the 'Sea Shanty' wall hanging showing it pinned to a softwood studio wall

Right:
'Hampton Court'. The inspiration for this closely knotted piece was a design of an Elizabethan knot garden. The ceramic plaques representing paths that bisect the various areas of plant-like knotting give this hanging a curiously heraldic quality. The knotting is carried out in shades of blue and green

Sculptures

These are free-standing three-dimensional structures which can be large enough to stand on the floor or, if smaller, on a shelf or table. They can be either self supporting using heavy, stiff rope and wrapping techniques, or be wholly or partially supported by armatures. The armature could be integrated into the sculpture by covering it with macramé, or be the focus and reason for a knotted decoration as in the ceramic and macramé head, 'Salome'.

Art Forms and Other Media

It should be obvious by now that the various other media used in combination with macramé could be easily incorporated into these art forms. A mobile of leather thonging would look spectacular if small pieces of fleece or laminated leather decorations were added. Various related found objects could be intermingled within a hanging reminding the observer of the impact that a particular scene had upon the artist. For example, 'Sea Shanty' evokes the feelings of the sea by showing the colours of the sea and the textures of nets as well as the pebbles and driftwood which are the natural representatives of the sea-shore.

Sculptures, hangings and mobiles are some of the best vehicles for displaying handmade beads and decorations and it is possible to make them in just the right size, colour and type for a construction that you are in the process of designing.

Pottery, papier mâché, objects trouvés, antique or new items can all be used in an artistic context, but do not allow the seemingly endless list of usable items to cause you to over-decorate. Restraint must be exercised in order to achieve a successful piece of craftwork executed with a sense of design and proportion. Study the various textures of the cords in relation to each other, the amount of space left in proportion to the knotting (it is not necessary or desirable to fill up every space with beads or baubles) and above all be selective in the use of added items. Two or three pebbles can create interest where rows of them could look dull or boring. No two people have the same likes and dislikes and in the end the only criterion must be your own taste, and if you are satisfied with your work that is really all that matters.

Project: 'Draco', a Dragon Mobile
Made in Wire and Cotton Twine

Originally a windsock was a pole with a carved dragon's head mounted on top of it, and a tube of cloth (which formed the body) was attached to the head. When the windsock was held aloft on its pole the tube filled with wind and caused the body of the dragon to writhe like a living creature.

During the latter part of the Roman empire the Roman armies used windsocks as banners and these dragons were considered to be the chief insignia of the legions. During a triumphal procession in Rome the dragons were described as embroidered in purple threads and fastened to the jewelled points of spears.

The design of this macramé dragon is based upon that of the windsock dragons. As he is made in an openwork pattern on a lampshade frame this dragon will not billow in the wind like his ancestors, but he still looks quite dramatic and awe-inspiring.

'Awake! for Morning in the Bowl of Night
Has flung the Stone that puts the Stars to Flight:
And Lo! the Hunter of the East has caught
The Sultan's Turret in a Noose of Light.'
The Rubaiyat of Omar Khayyam
trans. Edward Fitzgerald

'Hunter of the East', a beaded door curtain knotted in white cotton twine and decorated with many different kinds of bead

MATERIALS

2 hanks of green knitting (dish-cloth) cotton

1 large ball of stiff yellow macramé cord 2mm (⅛in) wide

Assortment of green cords all thicknesses and shades each 2m (2yd 7in) long (The

'Draco', a macramé dragon mobile, is worked on a lampshade frame and suspended from the ceiling on transparent nylon threads

allowance of green cotton is sufficient to cover this if you have no other green oddments.)

1 reel of bright green or brown rayon fishing twine, for the lead

1 small ball of thin yellow macramé twine, for the ears

6m (6yd 20in) thick 5mm (¼in) jute cord

2 globular glass beads, for the eyes

32 small barrel-shaped beads, for the ears

Assortment of different shaped green beads

9 yellow chenille-covered 30cm (1ft)-long wires, used in the making of paper flowers and obtainable in most craft shops.

1 small roll of millinery wire painted yellow

A 12-sectioned barrel-shaped lampshade frame painted yellow. (The frame used was 25cm (10in) long and 10cm (4in) in diameter at the ends.)

2 curtain rings 2.5cm (1in) in diameter

2 curtain rings 4cm (1½in) in diameter

1 curtain ring 5.5cm (2¼in) in diameter

METHOD

1 Cut the following lengths of cord:
   Yellow   42 cords 4.2m (4yd 21in) long
            2 cords 7m (7yd 24in) long
   Green   62 cords 2m (2yd 7in) long
            8 cords 8m (8yd 24in) long
   Jute   1 cord 4m (4yd 13in) long.

On the open end of the lampshade frame

2 Facing away from the frame to be worked outwards forming the head, attach 60 green cords 2m (2yd 7in) long by lark's head knots at their centres to the short wires of the frame, five cords to each section (120 working cords).

3 Mark one long bar of the frame as the top, A (see diagram 49), and in every section except the top two sections attach, by lark's head knots at their centres, four yellow cords 4.2m (4yd 21in) long to the short wires. These should lie along the frame so that the knots made with these cords will form

A fifteenth-century windsock dragon. Here the pole support has been replaced by a rope around the dragon's neck and resembles a kite more than a banner

the body (80 working cords). Thread these yellow cords in between the green cords as shown in diagram 50.

4 On the top two sections attach to the short wires in each section by lark's head knots at their centres one yellow cord 7m (7yd 24in) long, one yellow cord 4.2m (4yd 21in) long and four green cords 8m (8yd 24in) long (24 working cords). Mount these cords as shown in diagram 51.

5 Attach the 4m (4yd 13in) jute cord to the frame at B in diagram 49. Leave 2.5m (2yd 26in) on one side of the join with the short green cords and, using the

109

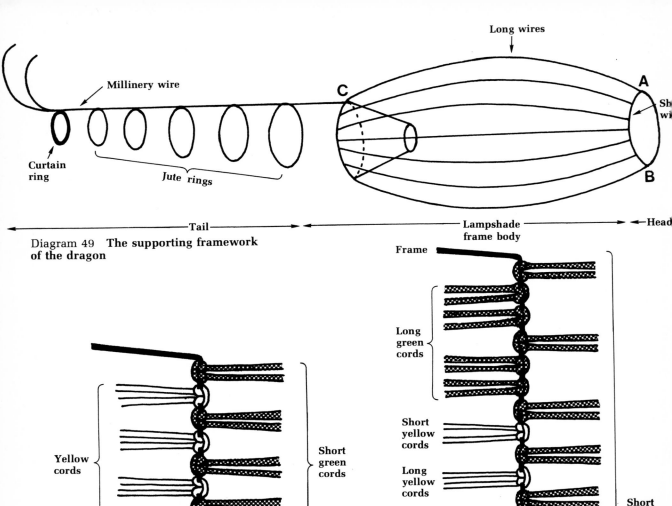

Diagram 49 **The supporting framework of the dragon**

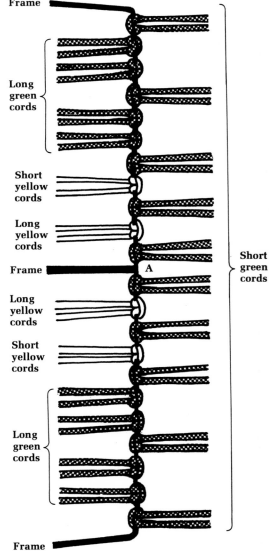

Diagram 50 **Dark threads are the green cords, light threads are yellow**

other 1.5m (1yd 23in) as a leader cord for the yellow and green cords that will form the body attached in stages 3 and 4, work two circular rows of horizontal cording over the lampshade frame. Trim off the end of the jute cord and glue the cut end behind the horizontal cording.

Diagram 51 **Top two sections of the lampshade frame**

110

Head

6 Return to the 120 green working cords and the 2.5m (2yd 26in) of the jute cord. Using the jute cord as a leader work three circular rows of horizontal cording outwards away from the frame.

7 In the next row of cording remove and cut off the ends of every fourth green cord. Work one row of cording.

8 Repeat stage 7 three more times. Cut off the end of the jute cord and secure it inside the head.

9 Attach one green cord 2m (2yd 7in) long at its centre on either side, at E and D (diagram 52), of the remaining small circular hole. Divide the remaining green cords down the centre, top A to bottom B, into two groups. Using the two cords formed by each 2m (2yd 7in) cord as working cords on either side and each group of cords as fillers, make two square-knot sinnets 10cm (4in) long.

10 Tie the two sinnets together at their ends and tuck the ends of the sinnets into the small corded hole. Leave the loose unknotted ends outside to form the dragon's moustache. Secure the sinnets and pull the top and bottom of the circle together with a stitch. Trim the moustache raggedly.

11 Wrap the 4cm (1½in) rings with an oddment of bright green cord and wrap the 2.5cm (1in) rings with an oddment of pale green cord. Sew the two bright green rings into the eye positions (see the photo of the head). Sew the pale green rings inside them and sew the globular glass eye beads into the centres of both rings. Make the eyelids and ears and sew into position.

Eyelids

12 Use the longer ends of green cord that were trimmed from the head. Use four cords together as a leader cord. Attach eight cords by lark's head knots at their centres to one end of the leader (16 working cords).

13 Work one row of horizontal cording; add two cords to each end of the next row of horizontal cording. Work another row. Trim off the ends of the leader cord and

glue under the eyelid. Trim working cords to a length of 1cm (⅜in) to form the eyelashes. Make two eyelids.

Ears

14 Onto a small working board pin eight thin yellow cords 2m (2yd 7in) long by their centres as shown in diagram 53. Drop 10cm (4in) down the cords and, using one outer cord as a leader, work the other 15 over it in a row of horizontal cording. Secure the leader with a bead and an overhand knot. Leave this cord hanging loose and, using the last cord worked as the leader, work another row of cording in the opposite direction, finishing this one too with a bead and an overhand knot.

15 Continue knotting horizontal cording rows in alternate directions, fastening off each leader with a bead and an overhand knot until all cords have been worked.

16 Trim the ends to a length of 15cm (6in). Cut the ends held by the pins in half and secure the ears to the dragon's head with these ends. The photo on p. 23 illustrating cording in Chapter 3 shows a dragon's ear.

Body

17 Return to the yellow and green cords that were set onto the lampshade frame and which have already had two rows of cording worked with them. The whole body from now on is worked in alternate square knots. For the first round, with the four long yellow cords at A tie a six-knot square-knot button (two working and two filler cords). Work the rest of this row and the next four circular rows with alternate square knots.

18 On the sixth round tie a six-knot button knot with each set of four green cords — four button knots in all — and continue alternate square knots for another four rows.

19 Repeat stages 17 and 18 until the lampshade is covered. Clove hitch all cords except the sixteen green cords and the eight yellow cords in the middle of them onto the short wires at the end of the frame.

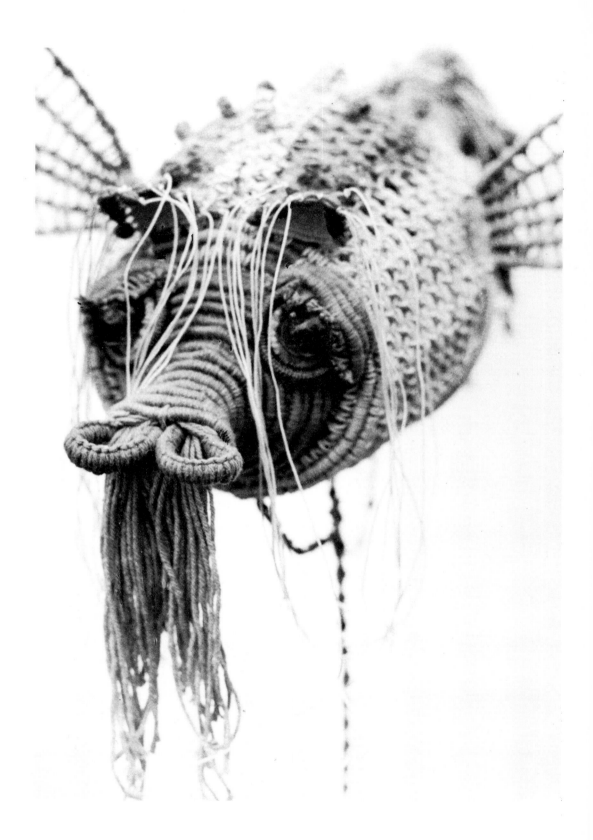

TOP

A

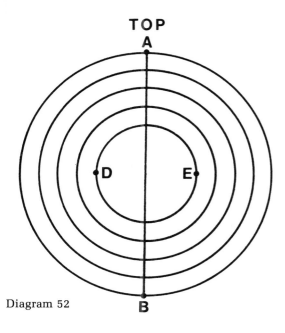

Diagram 52

B

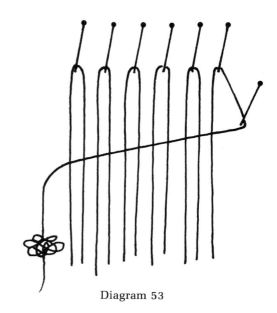

Diagram 53

Tail

20 Onto the light fixing inside the tail end of the lampshade frame secure at their centres as many 2m (2yd 7in) cords as will fit onto the circular fixing. Use as many oddments of different green cords as you can find; alternatively, use green cotton dish-cloth cord. Tuck these cords inside the frame out of the way for the time being.

21 Using the remaining 2m (2yd 7in) of jute cord make five double cord circles (see diagram 49) graded in size from the end of the lampshade frame to the large 5.5cm (2¼in) curtain ring.

The head of 'Draco' showing the positions of the eyes, eyelids and ears

22 On the top strut, between the long yellow cords, fasten at C in diagram 49 two pieces of millinery wire 50cm (1ft 8in) long. Using the yellow cords that have not been clove hitched to the frame make a square knot sinnet. Use the four short cords and the wire as fillers and the four long cords used double to make two as working cords. Continue the button knots making the same distance between them as on the body. Leave out the filler wire when tying these knots and use only four square knots to each button. Every 4cm (1½in) attach a cord circle to the sinnet, grading them downwards in size until the last circle knotted on is the large 5.5cm (2¼in) curtain ring. Leave short cords hanging.

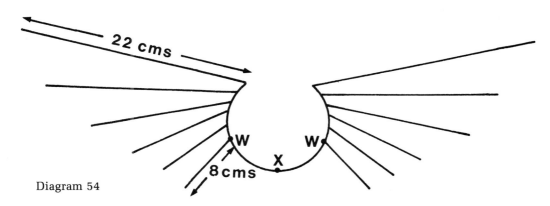

Diagram 54

113

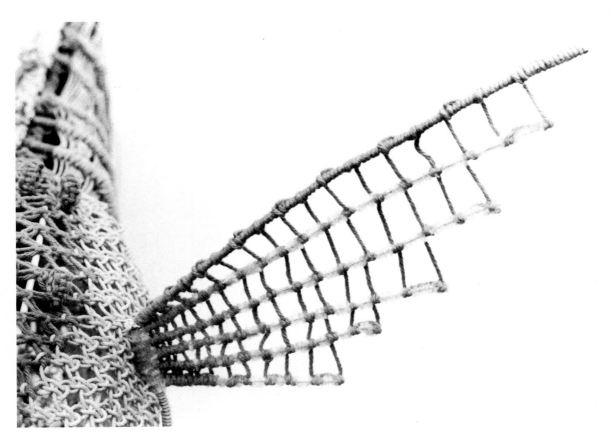

23 Separate the two wires beyond the curtain ring and tie a square knot sinnet (using two long yellow cords as working cords and the wire as a filler) on each wire. At the end of wire secure the sinnet with a touch of glue and leave cords hanging for approximately 70cm (28in). Finish each end with a bead and an overhand knot.

24 Make a square knot sinnet either side of the central yellow one using the green cords (four working cords used double to make two and four filler cords on each side). Continue the green button knots, four square knots in each button, leaving the same distance between each as on the body but remembering that now there will be only one on each side instead of two. Whenever the green sinnets reach a cord circle, clove hitch the cords to it. Continue until the green cords have been clove hitched to the curtain ring. Leave them hanging.

The wings, showing the density of the vertical cording

25 Using all the other yellow cords leave four floating cords, work a four cord square knot sinnet, leave four floating cords, etc., until at the underside of the tail two square-knot sinnets lie side by side. As you come to the cord circles clove hitch all cords except the filler cords to them, exchange filler and working cords and leave eight cords hanging loose at the bottom of each circle. Continue working this pattern until all the remaining cords are clove hitched onto the curtain ring.

26 Pull all the green cords tucked into the body of the lampshade frame through the tubular tail to hang out at the end. Pull some through the floating cords on the underside of the tail to hang with the yellow cords already there.

27 Trim all cords to varying lengths as shown in the photographs and finish each one off with a bead, a coil or an overhand knot.

Wings

28 Bend a piece of millinery wire 42cm (17in) long to the shape marked in diagram 54. Wrap 22cm (9in) of the wire at each end with green cord and the rest with yellow.

29 Cut and attach five chenille-covered wires to the millinery wire on each side as shown in diagram 54.

30 Using a small ball of green cord as a leader cord and starting at W, cover each wing with openwork vertical cording that is more open towards the edges, as shown in the photograph. Turn in the ends of the chenille wires to hold the leader cord in position at the ends of the wires. Fasten off the green leader cord when it reaches the end of the green wrapped cord.

31 Tie the wings into position around the widest part of the dragon's body using thin yellow twine and a curved upholstery needle.

The lead

32 Cut the fishing twine into the following lengths:
3 cords 2m (2yd 7in) long
1 cord 8m (8yd 24in) long
1 cord 1.8m (1yd 11in) long
1 cord 45cm (18in) long.

33 Attach at their centres one cord 2m (2yd 7in) long and one cord 8m (8yd 24in) long to the base of the wing section, X. Tie a 3cm (1¼in) bannister bar.

34 Attach the 45cm (18in) long cord and the 1.8m (1yd 11in) cord by their centres to the dragon's underside at the join of his head and body. Make a 15cm (6in) bannister bar. Join to the central bannister bar and continue the central bannister bar for another 3cm (1¼cm).

35 Attach the two 2m (2yd 7in) long cords at their centres to the dragon's underside at the join between the body and the tail. Using all four cords together knot a series of overhand knots for 22cm (9in). Join to the central bannister bar and continue the central bannister bar until it reaches a length of 1m (1yd 3in). Finish with an overhand knot.

36 Attach transparent nylon cords for hanging at A and C and at the curtain ring at the end of the dragon's tail.

Glossary

ARMATURE An internal support, usually made of metal or wood, for a piece of sculpture.

AWL A tool used to make stitching holes in leather.

BANNISTER BAR A spiral sinnet worked with a series of half knots.

BATT A small board or tile used as a support when making a pot.

BISCUIT The first firing of a piece of pottery.

BERRY KNOT A raised knot incorporating cording and square knots.

BERRY TASSEL A decorative tassel in the form of a berry.

BUTTERFLY BOBBIN A bobbin that loops up long ends of cord.

BUTTON KNOT Square knots looped to form a three-dimensional bead.

CHINESE CROWN KNOT A decorative knot that can be used by itself or in sinnets.

CLOVE HITCH A basic macramé knot.

COIL KNOT A decorative overhand knot.

EYED BEADS Beads with eye shaped decorations.

FILLER CORD The cords around which the knots are tied.

FLOATING CORDS Cords left unknotted.

FOIL BEAD Glass bead with foil added inside to give extra brightness and decoration.

FOOT-RING The ridge at the bottom of a pot that enables it to stand upright.

FOUNDATION CORD The mounting cord used to support the working and filler cords.

GESSO A smooth surface covering of whitening and glue used in papier mâché etc.

GLOST FIRING The glaze firing of a piece of pottery.

GRAPH PAPER Paper printed with measured squares.

LAPIS LAZULI A blue semi-precious stone.

LARK'S HEAD KNOT A knot used at the start of a piece of macramé.

LEADER CORDS The knot bearing cords used in horizontal and diagonal cording.

LOVERS' KNOT A decorative knot using two overhand knots.

LUSTRE GLAZE A glaze that features a metallic finish.

MILLIFIORI VENETIAN GLASS BEADS Highly patterned and coloured glass beads.

OXIDE A colouring agent used in pottery.

OVERHAND KNOT. A simple and widely used knot.

PENDANT BEAD A bead which has its threading hole at one end which enables it to hang downwards.

SINNET A chain of successive knots.

SQUARE KNOT One of the basic macramé knots, also called a flat knot.

SLIP Liquid clay.

SNAKED WHIPPING A variation of the wrap knot.

SUEDE SPLITS Thonging with a suede face on each side.

THUMP MAT Decorative mat used by sailors to protect the surface of the deck.

TURK'S HEAD KNOT. A tubular knot.

WHIRLER A revolving circular working table.

WORKING BOARD A stiff board used as a support for knotting.

WORKING CORDS The cords used for tying knots.

WRAP KNOT A knot used to hold cords together.

Suppliers

All of these suppliers are mail order
vendors. Most are international suppliers.

UK

Dryad, P.O. Box 38, Northgates, Leicester,
LE1 9BU, England. **Leather, twine and jute.
Excellent selection of beads.**

Lodge Enterprises, 23 Redan Place,
Queensway, London W2 4SA, England.
**Specialist yarns – silk, linen chenille,
tussah, llama, alpaca, camel and berber
wools.**

Mill Craft, Tay works, 23 Lochee Road,
Dundee, DD1 5AD, Scotland. **Good range of
coloured jutes and heavy polypropylenes.**

Podmore Ceramics Limited, 105 Minet Road,
London, SW9 7UH, England. **All ceramic
equipment including cold clay, plaster
moulds and sprig moulds.**

Texere Yarns, College Mill, Barkerend Road,
Bradford, West Yorkshire, BD3 9AQ,
England. **Comprehensive range of natural
coloured jutes, cottons and linens. Large
range of coloured wools.**

USA

Glues
Masters and wildwood Barge cement 100 Jacksonville Rd Towaco N.J. 07082

Weldwood contact cement U.S. Plywood Co
2305 Superior St Kalamazoo Mitch. 49003

Findings
Russo Leather and Findings Ltd 1460 East 4th
St Los Angeles Calif. 90052

Thonging
Roberta Creative Leathers
296 Donlea Barrington Ill. 60010

General
Sax Arts and Crafts 207 N. Milwaukee Wis.
53202

Index

Numbers in **bold** type refer to the page no. of the illustration

adhesives 18, 31
alternate square knots 21, **22**
animal fibres 15
armature 44, 47, **46**
awl 31

bag 79, 82–3, **78, 80, 81**
bannister bar 22
beads, attaching 64
    ceramic 60, 62, 63, 64, **59**
    cloisonné 67, **67**
    cold clay 64, **59**
    eyed **44, 58**
    firing 63
    foil **58**
    glass 60, **58**
    millifiori 57, **58**
    paper 64, **64**
    papier mâché 63, 64, **50, 58**
    plastic 60
    shapes **60**
    threading 64
    trade 57, **58**
    wood 62, **58**
bell 53, 89, **35, 37, 88–90**
belt 79, 80, **78, 81, 86**
berry knot 26, **26**
berry tassel 25, **25**
bird table 95, 98, **97**
biscuit 34–6
bones 62, **58**
bracelet 54, 69, 70, **44, 70**
butterfly bobbin 15, **15, 16**
button knot 22, **22**

cape **33**
Chatelain **52**
chenille 15, **14, 88**
chimes 89, **94**
chinese crown knot 26, **27**
circular knotting 28, **28**
clove hitch 23–4, **23–4**
clove orange **10**
coil knot 20, **20**
coiling 38, **39**

cold clay 38
collage **11**
cord sizes 15
cording 23–4, **23–4**
cotton 13, **14**
cradle 87, **87**
cross-wheel button 83
curtain 103, **16, 46, 66, 106**
cylinder 22

dish 96, **41, 95**
dog lead 79–80, **79**
double half hitch 23–4, **23–4**
dragon 107, 109, 111, 113–15, **108, 110, 112–15**

earring 54, **70**
earthenware 34–5, **37**
ethnic objects 51–3, **52**
evening wear 79

filler cords 19
firing 34–6
flat knot 21, **21**
fleece 15, 54, **51, 54**
floating cords 19
fly fringe 84–6, **84, 85**
foot-ring 87
foundation cords 19
fringes 10 16

gesso 48
glazes 35–6, **37, 41**
glost firing 35

half hitch knot 23, **23**
half knot 21, **21**
hangings, ceramic 18, 105, **101**
    construction **102, 104**
    flat 101, 103, **54, 105**
    leather **32, 34**
    relief 101, 103, **56**
house plants 87

incising 48

jute 13, **14**

lampshade 107–15, **34**
lapis lazuli 57
lark's head knot 20, **20**
leader cords 19
leather, laminated 32, **33**
   punch 31
   sinnet cover **31**
   tools 20
   types of 20
linen 13, **14**
linocuts 40, **41, 42**
lovers' knot 26, **27**

man made object 51–3
masks 56, **36, 57**
measure 15
mobiles 103, 107–15, **101, 108**
monkey's fist knot **12**

natural materials 53–4, 62, **58**
necklace 54, 67–9, **30, 61, 67–71**

overdress **72**
overhand knot 20, **20**

paper pulp 43–4, 48
papier mâché 43–4, **44, 45, 46**
   decoration 48
   finish 50
paring 31, **32**
pebbles 53, 62, 67, **58**
pewter **32**
pins 17–18
plackets 72
plant hangings 87–9, **43, 50, 88, 91, 93, 94**
plant pots, brass **55**
   ceramic 90–4, 38–40, 87–9, **39, 40, 91**
   papier mâché 44–7, **43, 50**
plaster of paris 63
plastic rings 54, 97
polyester 15, **14**
polypropylene 15, **14**
pomander **10, 18, 38**
poncho **18**
porcelain 35, **37**
press moulding 62–3, **62**

raku 36, **36**
rayon 15, **10, 14**
reversed lark's head knot 20
rosaries 57

safety ruler 31
saucer dish 40, 45, 47, 92–4, **45, 47, 93, 94**

sculpture 107, **103**
seeds 53, 62, 67, **58**
shells 53, 62, 67, **58**
sieve **91**
silk 15, **14**
silver **30, 54, 67, 71**
sinnet 19
sisal 13, **14**
slab building 39–40
sleeve **77**
slip 40, **41**
snaked whipping 25, **25**
sprig mould 93
square knot 21, **21**
stoneware 35, **35, 37**
suede 30–1
suede splits 31
supports, curtain 16
   table 16
   three-dimensional articles 28, **28**
surrealism 51
synthetic fabrics 15

tables 95, 97–100, **49, 95, 97**
tabletops, ceramic 39–40, **41, 42**
   papier mâché 47, **48**
   wood 97, **95**
tassels 25, **25**
terracotta 34, 35, **37, 41, 42**
terylene 15, **14, 18**
thonging 31–3
thump mat 50
tracing paper **24**
triple knot 22
tunic 73, **29, 73**
turk's head knot 27, **26, 70**
twine 13, **14**
twisted sinnet 22

undercutting 47, **47**

varnish 50
vegetable fibres 13
vegetable ivory **57**

waistcoat 74–7, **74, 75**
waterproofing 50
whirler 39, **39**
windsock 107, **109**
wool 15, **14**
working board 16, **17, 18**
working cords 19
wrap knot 25, **25**

yarns 13–15, **14**